A TREE FULL OF ANGELS

A TREE
FULL OF ANGELS

Seeing the Holy in the Ordinary

Macrina Wiederkehr, OSB

HarperSanFrancisco
An Imprint of HarperCollins*Publishers*

The author gratefully acknowledges permission to reprint: From "The Victory" from Thomas Merton, *Collected Poems*. Copyright © 1946 by New Directions Publishing Corporation. From "The Victory" from Thomas Merton, *The Collected Poems of Thomas Merton*, Laurence Pollinger Limited. From "The Tyger" and "Auguries of Innocence" from William Blake, *The Poetry and Prose of William Blake*, edited by David V. Erdman, copyright © 1970, Doubleday & Company, Inc. From "Renascence" by Edna St. Vincent Millay. From *Collected Poems*, Harper & Row. Copyright © 1912, 1940 by Edna St. Vincent Millay. Reprinted by permission. From "Reluctance" in *Collected Poems of Robert Frost*, by Robert Frost, Holt and Company, 1930. From "Reluctance" in *The Poetry of Robert Frost*, by Robert Frost, edited by Edward Connery Lathem. Permission granted by Estate of Robert Frost and Jonathan Cape Ltd.

All scripture quotations, unless otherwise noted, are from the Jersualem Bible, ed. Alexander Jones (Garden City, NY: Doubleday & Co., 1968). All poetry for which credit is not given is by Macrina Wiederkehr. Excerpts from letters in chapter 8 are used by permission of the correspondents.

FIRST HARPERCOLLINS PAPERBACK EDITION PUBLISHED IN 1990

Library of Congress Cataloging-in-Publication Data

Wiederkehr, Macrina.
   A tree full of angels: seeing the holy in the ordinary / Macrina Wiederkehr.
     p. cm.
   Includes bibliographic references.
   ISBN: 0–06–254868–9 (cloth)
   ISBN: 0–06–250495–9 (pbk.)
   1. Spiritual life–Catholic authors. I. Title
[BX2350.2W533 1990]   90–32475
248.3—dc20   CIP

---

95 96 97 98 99 RRD(H) 10 9 8 7 6 5 4 3 2 1

In memory of my parents
whose poverty has enriched me
and taught me to gather up the crumbs

and

To Tami and Janine
who stayed with me during a dream
as the crumbs became loaves

CONTENTS

CONTENTS

ACKNOWLEDGMENTS

Beautiful places help to nurture creativity.
For much of the inspiration in this book, I owe thanks to:

The Desert House of Prayer of Cortoro, Arizona

for the desert hills, where I found enough solitude to remember my childhood

for the poetry of the cactus—from thorns to blossoms

for the silence of my cell, which taught me more than I could hold

for the vision and courage of Father John Kane, who believed that seeds could grow in the desert.

Serra Retreat of Malibu, California

for the Franciscans and their kindness to me during my stay

for the wordless prayers of the mountains and the music of the ocean

for the dolphins with their constant reminder that life is a festival.

Our own Hesychia House of Prayer in Arkansas

for the wide-open meadows and the rolling hills

for the bluebirds and the goldfinches and every winged thing that fills the day with song

for the whippoorwill—its lonely call and its faithful night watch

for Sister Louise Sharum's belief that this holy place was in God's design.

Caring people help books to be born.
For these caring people I give thanks:

Sister Cabrini Schmitz and Sister Scholastica Vogelpohl of my
   community
Anne Marie Candido of the University of Arkansas

   for their many hours of reading my manuscript
   for their insights and suggestions.

My Benedictine community

   for the love, support, and affirmation I have received from
   my sisters
   for the gift of my desert sabbatical.

My sister, Ann,

   for leading me to Harper & Row.

INTRODUCTION

A spiritual awakening is taking place in the world today. An authentic yearning to touch the depths of who we are is urging people to seek out ways to rekindle the soul. And everywhere one hears talk of angels! It is understandable that we should be drawn to the mystical, for implanted in us is a seed of the divine. Although this yearning for the infinite is a promising sign for the spiritual growth of this age, a few cautionary flags wave in my mind's eye.

I am concerned about the many people today who are lured to extraordinary spiritual phenomena that are manifested, it seems to me, in sensational ways. Stories abound about visions and trances, weeping statues, rosaries turning gold. Celestial beings are emerging everywhere, and angels are in danger of becoming trendy. The fast pace of our lives makes it difficult for us to find grace in the present moment, and when the simple gifts at our fingertips cease to nourish us, we have a tendency to crave the sensational.

A second concern is this: As we pine for angels and the otherworldly, there is the danger of missing a precious aspect of Christianity. We are an incarnational people. The Word was made flesh in our midst. We are rooted in an earth that God has proclaimed good. Here on this good earth we have become flesh with the seed of God hidden in us. The greatest of all visions is to see Christ, indeed, to see God, in the frail and glorious human family of the world. It is not always easy, but hope tenders that which is difficult. Pierre Teilhard de Chardin says it well: "Creatures are all around me with their disappointing weaknesses and their terrifying powers."

Ah, yes! It is true. We have within us terrifying powers for good and for evil. This book is about trusting the power for good.

It is for people who long for spiritual depth and have the courage to struggle with the eternal questions that rise in their hearts. In my heart, too, there is an infinite longing, an ache for what is otherworldly. Although I have never seen an angel, I am surrounded by a sacred presence I cannot explain.

This book is not about the sensational. It is about bringing the longings of your heart to the present moment and finding the grace that waits for you there. It is about finding the sacred in the ordinary. You are to gather up the joys and sorrows, the struggles, the beauty, love, dreams and hopes of every hour that they may be consecrated at the altar of daily life.

This book has clamored for my heart's attention. It has been an ache in my heart, an ache not for a book but for God. The book is just a way to talk with you about it. Much of this work is autobiographical, and so it is very personal. I write about the "disappointing weaknesses and the terrifying powers" of my own life. In giving you this book I am giving you my heart.

There is a yearning deep in the human heart—so deep is it an ache within. An ache for God! This book is about how to embrace and celebrate this ache for God rather than ignoring it or denying it.

We live under the eye of God. There is no escape from that loving gaze. There is only one way for this ache in us to be healed, and that is in becoming like God. When we meet God face to face, without dying, there will be no ache left . . . only joy. This will take until heaven, but heaven begins right where we are. Holiness is within our grasp, at our fingertips.

The first heaven we experience is when we become aware that we live under the eye of God. The question we must ask our heart is, "Am I comfortable under the eye of God? Or is God getting too close?" We are strange and lovely creatures. We can ache for God tremendously yet find ourselves getting nervous if God gets too close. After all, the closer God gets, the more we hear the call to be divinized. It is both exciting and frightening to hear that call. Being divinized is still part of the unknown, even though it is our baptismal invitation. We prefer to keep the comfortable masks that we know rather than to go through the purifying process of becoming like God.

In these meditations I will reflect with you on this ache for God that lives in every heart. The gift we have to bring to this ache is our frailty and our splendor. Both must be embraced to find the saving grace that keeps us from death. The ache in our heart needs to be fed. Crumbs are entirely sufficient. Crumbs are those small things that the world would toss aside, seeing little value in them. However, to the one who lives under the eye of God, they are far from valueless. This book will harvest the crumbs. It will lovingly gather them up for the banquet of daily life. It will proclaim the good news that for the person who has learned to see with inner eyes there are no leftovers. Everything in life can be nourishing. Everything can bless us, but we've got to be there for the blessing to occur. Being present with quality is a decision we are invited to make each day. It is another way to become like God. Due to the reality of our terribly distracted, cluttered, and noisy existence, the decision for real presence is not easy. If we can make this decision and live it, it will be a kind of salvation for us. It can save us from many kinds of death: the death of apathy and mediocrity, the death of carelessness, the death of boredom, the death of selfishness, the death of meaningless. There is nothing so healing in all the world as real presence. Our real presence can feed the ache for God in others.

This is a book about seeing and harvesting. Seeing the holy in the ordinary! Harvesting angels out of the crumbs! Spending your days in the fast lane of life impairs the quality of your seeing. If you want to see to the depths, you will need to slow down. You live in a world of theophanies. Holiness comes wrapped in the ordinary. There are burning bushes all around you. Every tree is full of angels. Hidden beauty is waiting in every crumb. Life wants to lead you from crumbs to angels, but this can happen only if you are willing to unwrap the ordinary by staying with it long enough to harvest its treasure.

It is time to harvest:

- a spider web, wearing the morning's dew
- a mistake, reflected upon and learned from
- reconciliation after a quarrel
- an autumn tree letting go of her leaves
- a spring tree putting leaves on again
- a wound, embraced and understood.

The question remains. Will I be there? Will I be there with my open eyes? Will I unwrap the gift of the ordinary? Will I gather up the crumbs? Will I harvest the angels hidden in those crumbs?

The incredible gift of the ordinary! Glory comes streaming from the table of daily life. Will I be there to catch the rays or will I remain blind to the holy because I'm too busy to see? Am I too busy with my own agenda to let God's agenda bless me?

One of the treasures I am intent on helping you harvest in your life is the seed of your own goodness, your possibility for splendor. For this reason I was delighted when one of my sisters led me to an old book by Raoul Plus, a Jesuit, entitled *Dust, Remember Thou Art Splendor*. Since these reflections were nearly finished when I discovered the book, it felt like a confirmation of the hidden treasure of our splendor that I was trying to uncover. Upon reading it I immediately sat down and prayed to its dear old author. I asked a blessing on the contents of this book and all its readers. Experiences such as this are experiences of God's presence. They ought not to be taken lightly. We need to trust not only God's spirit, but the good spirits of all those who have died in Christ and those who are living in Christ right now. And so, whether Father Plus is still living in this life or alive in eternity, his spirit has brushed across my spirit. I am blessed, and so are you.

This brings me to the heart of this book, which is trusting the God who speaks to us in our experiences at every moment. No one ever gave me permission to trust my own experience as prayerful and holy. It was something I stumbled upon, like a treasure hidden in a field. From earliest childhood my life has been shot through with God. Childhood did not bless me with adults I could talk with about these experiences, so often my experiences went unnamed. I am only now beginning to name them and let them bless me. It is wonderful how the past can still bless and heal us. Pain from the past can be healed. Joy from the past can still touch us into new life. What I remember most about my past is that I lived for so long with this unnamed ache.

There are two qualities from my childhood that linger in my memory. I had an insatiable desire to know, yet I didn't automatically believe everything I was taught. I always asked questions, though more often in the depths of my soul than aloud. My desire for knowledge and my yearning for the truth encouraged me to spend lots of time with my soul. It is there I found the ache.

This ache, quite naturally, led me to wonder about other people. What did they do with that yearning in their hearts? What did they call it? How did they feed it? And so began my journey to the "experts" on the spiritual life. I began reading all I could find by the great spiritual guides of the past. I have been through the writings of John of the Cross, Teresa of Avila, and Ignatius of Loyola. John Cassian has been a favorite desert friend. Saint Basil the Great and Gregory of Nyssa, brothers of Saint Macrina, have often blessed me. I have devoured the rule of Saint Benedict. I have read the letters of John Chapman. The wisdom of the desert fathers and mothers has been a source of nourishment, as have the ancient writings of the *Philokalia*. I have found much to feed my ache in Julian of Norwich and Catherine of Siena. Teresa of the Child Jesus, a favorite of childhood days, has left her mark on my life. Perhaps more than any of the other spiritual classics, *The Cloud of Unknowing* has brought me closest to my center. Thomas Merton, who seems a twin to my soul with his restless, contemplative spirit, has touched me deeply. Dom Marmion, a favorite from novitiate days, still encourages me.

The list could go on and on. Other people and their passionate search for God have given me hope on my journey. Their writings have nourished me along the way. I feel the strength of this great cloud of witnesses, named in Heb. 12:1, surrounding me. They urge me on. They bless my search.

And yet, the ache lives on. What more can I say? I have been to the experts, but the ache lives on.

In recent years I seem to hear God say, "Put your books away. Be with me. Trust your experience. There are no experts in prayer, only people who have been faithful to the ache." I reflect on this with both anxiety and joy. Why shouldn't our experiences be filled with God? Who do we think it is who is breathing in us? Where do we think this ache has come from? And has it ever crossed our minds that God, too, has a deep yearning for us? This is the only message I've been receiving in prayer these days: "Forget the experts for a while. Trust your own experience."

Trusting our own experience is not nearly as easy as it sounds. We have not been brought up to trust our experience; we have been encouraged to listen to "the ones who know." If this book does anything at all for you, I hope that it will lead you to the awesome resources in your own soul.

You are a dwelling place for the Source of All Life. You are an offspring of the One who said, "I Am who Am." If the One who gave you birth lives within you, surely you can find some resources there in your sacred Center. An expert lives within you. An expert breathes out of you. Are you able to be still enough to become intimate with the One who lives within? This is the only expert you will ever meet. Your life is entwined with the God who gave you birth.

Frail dust, remember, *you are splendor!*

1. Little–Great–One, Come Home

A name is a precious gift. It is something to be lived into. It is someone to come home to. Your name is a word filled with the power of *you*. Call people by name shortly after you've met them and see how they come alive. Being able to name something or someone gives you a certain power and responsibility for it, for him, for her. Being able to name the ache in your life gives you power over that ache. Being able to name a fear in your life gives you power over the fear. Claiming and naming is part of life's experience.

The name you are given at baptism is a Word of God that you grow into. As your life unfolds you give new meaning to that name. It becomes yours more fully. It becomes *you*.

Sometimes we are given a new name to celebrate a call to a more radical way of life. The new name is a reminder of the new person we are to become. Abram becomes Abraham. Jacob becomes Israel. Saul becomes Paul. Martha Ann becomes Macrina.

Sometimes, by chance or by grace, we stumble upon a new name. It comes to us out of our life's experience. It is a name known only to us who receive it. In this book I am giving you a new name. Your new name comes out of my search for the meaning of my own name.

Recently I asked someone who knows Greek to search out the meaning of the name Macrina. He wrote back to tell me he had not been all that successful. He wasn't sure about my name. He thought the first part of the name meant great; and *ina* being a term of endearment, he came up with Little-Great-One. As I read those words, Little-Great-One, something clicked inside me. Like a flash of lightning it came to me: That's everybody's name! That's the answer to our lost identity. We are

. . . God's *anawim* of the Old Testament (Zeph. 3:12–20)
. . . the beloved, enfolded ones of the book of Hosea (Hos. 11:3–5)
. . . poor storm-tossed creatures, yet precious stones (Isa. 54:11–12)
. . . the poor little blessed ones of the Beatitudes (Matt. 5:1–11)
. . . earthenware jars filled with a treasure (2 Cor. 4:7)
. . . those who have nothing, yet possess everything (2 Cor. 6:10).

That's us! Little-Great-Ones!

The tragedy is that we keep forgetting the second part of our name, the great and glorious, precious stone part. As I was pondering this theme of littleness and greatness I suddenly remembered that my last name, Wiederkehr, means return again. In an instant my heart became full of prayer. It was as though God started praying within me, "Little-Great-One, come home."

Home! Come home! Does not this ache that refuses to leave our hearts want to remind us that we are not yet at home? What gifts do we possess to help us on this homeward journey except our littleness and our greatness, our frailty and our splendor, our poverty and our wealth, our new name, lived out. Little-Great-One, come home.

What is home but that place where your name becomes precious, the place where your name finds its power? You find power when you are at home because it is there that you are loved, cherished, and accepted just as you are, with all your frailty, fears, and flaws. It is there in that lovely dwelling place called home that you discover you don't have to be perfect to be loved. There, at home, you are able to embrace the truth that it's part of your life's journey to be in process. You don't have to be finished to be good. You don't have to be finished to see your splendor.

What is home but that place where forgiveness stands at the door, peers out the window, and rushes down the steps to meet you? You may be thinking, "I've never felt that kind of home." Well, neither have I, but I've experienced enough of home's moments to know that it's possible. It takes a lot of the real presence of *being there* to feel at home; sadly, many of us seldom feel at home.

The call from God is to come home, to embrace both our littleness and our greatness and come home. Come home to our families, our friends, our church, our selves, our God.

Where are the places you feel at home? Have you ever really felt at home? Do you ever feel like running away from home? Have you ever heard a call from deep within to come back home?

Running away from home is not all that uncommon. Sometimes we run away from home without leaving. We just conveniently aren't there for others. It hurts too much to be there and so we disappear. It is easy to disappear. Disappearing is what makes home so hard to find. People do it all the time. We disappear because we are uncomfortable with being in process.

Since I do not remember the home of my mother's womb, my first conscious home was the family into which I was born. That home was my first place of formation. I have cherished memories of my parents, brothers and sisters, the country, gardens, pine trees, grape vineyards, homemade bread and wine, poverty, faith, God, Sunday afternoons. It was not a home where I received everything I needed, but it was enough to get me started.

While I was living in this home I didn't understand it very well. It often takes a backward, reflective glance to understand the depths of things. It is catching up to me a little more each day, this first home of mine, and I am becoming aware of all the little ways I ran away from that home even while living in it. I disappeared a lot as a child. It was a creative way of surviving. I ran away to the forest that surrounded our farm. It became a place of solitude for me, a second home tucked away in the green of the trees.

Not all running away is harmful. Sometimes it is a necessary part of growth. Even now I'm discovering ways that I return to that first home. There is a child in me who needs to be embraced again and again. The reason for my flight as a child came from a wisdom I was too young to understand. Now in my later years I can harvest the wisdom of my childhood. I treasure those precious roots knowing that I have grown wings and I must move on. I must let go.

That first home is one that all of us must let go of as we go forth to find new homes. And yet, we always carry it with us. We are all we've ever been as we move forward, in process, to become all we can be. Going home is a sacred journey. We carry our names with us as we go.

Another important home for me is simply the hearts of friends. We all need those people in our lives whose acceptance, understanding, and love for us creates an atmosphere that feels like home, one of those places we can take off our shoes and be called by our first name. Friends are good stopping places when we've run away from home. They allow us to rest in our confusion, regain new strength as we gather up the crumbs needed to go back home, or perhaps move on to build a new home.

I come now to one of my most cherished homes of all, the Church, the Body of Christ on earth. The Church is that home into which I have been initiated, in which I have been anointed, healed, forgiven, nourished, and nurtured. The Church is that home where my formation continues, where I am transformed and divinized. She is a nurturing womb in which I have owned the responsibility to be in process.

The Church is also that home where I am often disappointed. She seems, at times, so slow to be wise. She has become complicated, so unlike the simple Christ of the Gospels. We call her Mother; theologically this is correct, yet living within her I sense a dilemma. Mother Church's dominant male leadership makes it difficult, at times, to find the *Mother* in her. It is an unfortunate imbalance and a failure Jesus would want us to own as we go forward into the future.

I am aware of the many ways the Church has failed me, and I have failed her. Yet in the midst of these mutual failures, I claim this Church as mine. She is my Church, my home, my mother. I will not run away from her, for I have seen through the cracks of her frailty her tremendous splendor, her littleness and her greatness, her poverty and her wealth. I feel more fed than failed. Not everyone can say this, however, and so we are called to great sensitivity in this area. Together we have to accept both the burden and the grace of being Church. The Church is us. She is mine and she is me. She is yours and she is you. She is home, a broken home, yes! Broken, because you and I are broken.

My monastic community is another special home in my life. It is that place where I live in gentle protest against the values of this world. It is that place where I try to help build a new home based on values that endure. It is the home I have most often almost run away from. Being made up of human beings, this community has a lot of human nature present, and what is human nature but a strange mixture of care and carelessness. In my impatient moments I tend to judge my community for not living up to the ideals we promised. With grace I am led to see that the only person I can judge, with God's help, is myself. I slowly come to understand that part of what is keeping my community from being all that it can be is my own lack of love, my own carelessness with God's love and the love and struggles of my sisters. Seeing us in process and being able to value our incompleteness has been for me a great means of grace. Saved, then, from my own impetuousness, I have been able to appreciate the truth that this monastic community is one of the homes God has given me. I do not regret having stayed with this community, in spite of its weaknesses.

There is also that home that I am to myself. Am I comfortable in the home that I call *me*? This home is of utmost importance, for it holds the key to my being comfortable in other homes. If I am not at home with myself I won't feel at home anywhere else. It is such a delight to come home to myself, to become my own friend. I experienced this kind of homecoming once when I was living alone. Under the guise of ministering to others I had become alienated from myself. In my everyday maddening ministerial rush I suddenly discovered myself eating on the run—grabbing a sandwich and eating it while standing up or going out the door. The violence of this great irreverence to myself suddenly occurred to me. I was not at home with myself. It took a while to slow down, but I was finally able to make a decision to spend time with myself. I began to experience the joy of being with *me*. I put a flower on the table, lit a candle, turned on soft music, ate slowly. I learned the joy of simply being with myself without rushing. It was like taking myself out to dinner. It was a kind of coming home to myself. When you can lovingly be present to yourself, your presence to others takes on a deeper quality also.

There are many ways we are called to come home to ourselves. There is that part of ourselves that feels ugly, deformed, unacceptable. That part, above all, we must learn to cherish, embrace, and call by name. A dream I once had helped me to see the importance of embracing myself and naming my fears.

I was with a group of friends. We were running from a fierce and fast-pursuing buffalo. There was an unusual closeness, a wonderful unity that existed among those of us who were running. We were all dreadfully fearful but immensely concerned about each other. It was as though we were all only one. We were that much united. We took shelter in an old abandoned house. I seemed to be the leader of the group that was fleeing. I stood at the window peering through the lattice, knowing full well what it was I had to do. The buffalo was waiting outside, pawing the ground. I knew that in order to get the buffalo to stop pursuing us I had to go out and face it. Rather than run from it I had to walk toward it. I had to look it in the face. I had to embrace it and invite it into the house. I went to the door. My hand was on the knob. When I awoke I was trying to get up enough courage to walk out of the house and go forth to meet the buffalo. I knew that I had to touch it to become its friend.

That buffalo was my life with all its fears. I had to face it and embrace it. This indeed is coming home to yourself, to face yourself and embrace yourself. Invite yourself into your own abandoned house, abandoned only because you are not at home with yourself. Invite yourself in, then. Sit down at table with your estranged self, estranged only because you've forgotten the real unity that exists within you. That unity was portrayed in my dream by the closeness that I felt with those who were fleeing with me.

So, invite yourself in! Treat that self like a beloved member of your household. It is a beloved member. It is *you*! You've come home.

In the beautiful image of being at home with yourself I am reminded of Jacob coming into an awareness of the holiness of the place where God visited him (Gen. 28:16–17). Still touched with the presence of the Divine after the memory of his dream, he cries out, "Truly, Yahweh is in this place and I never knew it! . . . This is nothing less than a house of God; this is the gate of heaven!" The memory of Jacob's intimate discovery becomes even more intimate for me as I begin to realize that each of us, as we come into awareness of our very self being a dwelling place for the Divine, can echo Jacob's cry in speaking of the self that we are, "Truly this is the house of God, the gateway to heaven." Not only do we come home to ourselves but we discover that the self we've come home to is a home for God. It was not an abandoned house after all. What an awesome discovery. I am a home for the Most High. How often after long periods of self-rejection, standing in my own abandoned house, I, too, cry out with new-found awareness, "Truly God was in this place all the while and I never knew it."

This brings me quite naturally to the home that God is becoming for me. Some people call it heaven. It begins here on earth. Heaven is a process. It is for this union with God that we were born. Much of this book is about this homecoming, the ache for God that leads us home. There is so much here on earth that can be the beginning of heaven for us. We live daily with the exciting possibility of meeting God face to face.

All of the homes I have mentioned—family, friends, church, community, self—are tinged with heaven. They are gateways to heaven. They have the potential of leading me more deeply into the heart of God. All of these homes, including the heart of God, are homes that I am sometimes tempted to run from. I run away from home. I return home. It is the way of the human heart. I run from what I desire most. I disappear for a while because I cannot bear to embrace the brokenness and uncertainty that is a part of the process of homecoming.

Sometimes it feels more like I am driven from home. There is that Hansel and Gretel aspect of me that feels forced to leave a cherished home because of the evil stepmother within me claiming there is not enough nourishment for both of us. If I don't go, she will starve. And she's probably right. That evil stepparent is my false self. There will never be enough nourishment for my false self. She has a colossal appetite. It is understandable that she, thinking only of self, tries to drive me away. And yet, she is the one who must go, for she is false. This evil stepparent exerts a tremendous power over my life. She takes advantage of my littleness. That littleness is really a blessing, but because I have not matured sufficiently to recognize the blessedness of littleness, I allow it to intimidate me. I listen to the false self and allow myself to be driven from home. That evil stepparent often succeeds in driving me from my family, my friends, my church, my community, myself, my God.

Farfetched as it all may sound, this favorite fairy tale from childhood days does sound like my own story. There are days when someone inside me seems to be shouting, "Leave your community; you'll never find the love you really need to grow there. Leave your church; it has lost the vision of the simple Christ." I am even, in some strange way, asked to leave myself. I do that by not believing in my gifts, by comparing myself to others, by allowing discouragement to control me. Every invitation to self-pity is an invitation to leave the home of myself. Every time I reach out to embrace power, people, possessions in an exclusive kind of way, I leave myself a little. I become a little more lost and in need of homecoming.

But all is not lost. For secretly I've remembered that it's truth I want, not lies. Like Hansel and Gretel I dropped crumbs along the way, hoping, often subconsciously, to find my way back home. The crumbs are the memories of all the good that was mine at home, of all the good that was mine even in a home that was not perfect. My time of being lost, those times when the birds ate the crumbs, turns out in the end to be a marvelous time of growth for me. On the way home I discover both my need and my strength. Coming home is a process. I find the way *on the way*. Eventually, in the midst of being lost, I gain the strength, like Gretel, to shove the witch into the oven, to take charge of my true self and rescue Hansel, and others including myself, from the clutches of evil, the false self. Violent as all of this may sound, it is a very good symbol of what actually happens in the conversion process. Scripture often uses the symbol of the furnace as that place where gold is tried, where our lives are tested, burning away what is dross and strengthening and making pure what is good. Jesus came to cast a fire on the earth; all that is preventing us from being at home in our own and God's heart must be burned away.

Fairy tales and myths have often been used as vehicles to teach a truth that is too deep for ordinary words. Our invitation to become one with God is too deep for ordinary words. How do we talk about a call to be like God? The early Christians were much more concerned about being divinized than about keeping laws. Sadly, somewhere along our historical journey we got preoccupied with law and doing things that would keep us out of hell. We lost sight of our original union with God and the continuing call to be like God. In fact, we became so busy keeping out of hell that we forgot we were on the way to heaven. We started loving God for the gifts we would receive or the punishment we would avoid. But is that truly love? What about the wonder and possibility of being simply and utterly in love, the only reason being that once upon a time before a burning bush the One Who Is said, "I Am who Am!" The bush still burns. What about our love? How bright is the flame?

All flames start out little. Do you remember when you were a little flame? Do you remember the poverty of your simple beginnings? Do you remember the moment when you, too, could say, "I am"? I am a little flame, but, at least, I *am*. Yes, that is where we began a long time ago. We began with nothing except our *I am*, and even that had to be said for us. That moment of littleness was cause for celebration. It was our birth.

Do you remember when you were born? What did you have to boast of then? What freedom! To be so little that you protested not when good was being done for you! You did not refuse when gifts were being given to you. There was such a moment of receptivity. That was long ago at your beginning, from the moment of your conception until your birth, and even after your birth until you were no longer content with being little. You were no longer able to experience your poverty with acceptance. You began to fight it and despair of it, and so your littleness lost its tremendous power and meaning. It became something to deny and run from rather than a way of being, a stance of life to be embraced and understood, thus making it possible for you to live with open hands, as a beggar waiting for each moment's new gifts.

Every gift we receive feeds the little flame that we are. Recognizing the need for our littleness to be fed turns us into grateful people. We learn at a very early age to take off our shoes and stand in wonder. It delights God to see our tiny flame yearning to be fed, to be ignited.

It is pure gift to be able to recognize our littleness as valuable. We are a treasure waiting to be discovered. We are often the very last to discover the treasure of ourselves. The gospel tells a story of someone who discovers a treasure hidden in a field and rushes out to buy the whole field (Matt. 13:44). You are that treasure, that precious stone; to find the treasure that you are, you must purchase the whole field of your life. It is only in embracing the whole field of yourself with all your frailty and poverty included that you will ever be able to find your true self. Your true self is hidden in the field of your life. That's why God didn't hesitate to purchase the field of your life with the blood of Jesus. We have been bought at a great price. We are offspring of the One who said, "I Am!" Our little "I am" is important to the great "I Am." We are on our way to greatness, for nothing can stop a flame.

We are not the only ones with an ache in our hearts. God's ache for us is immense. Listen to God's ache in my paraphrase of Hosea 11:3–4, 8:

I myself taught Ephraim to walk, I held them in my arms, but they did not know that I was caring for them, that I was leading them with human ties, with strings of love. . . . I was like someone lifting an infant . . . Ephraim, how could I part with you? Israel, how could I give you up?

What God most longs to discover in us is our willingness to embrace ourselves as we are at our beginning—empty, little, and poor. Our willingness gives God free space within us to work out the Divine Plan. Our potential for greatness is tremendous. Acceptance of our littleness makes it possible for our greatness to emerge. Our littleness is not a choice. It is simply the way we are. Our greatness, however, is a choice. When we choose to accept the life God has given to us, when we allow God to fill our emptiness, we are choosing greatness. Who can deny our call to greatness? Who can deny our call to be saints? Look at us!

> . . . Called before the world began, to be holy (Lev. 11:45; Eph. 1:4)
> . . . to be holy as God is holy (1 Pet. 1:15)
> . . . bearing within us the same mighty power that raised Jesus from the dead (Eph. 1:18–21)

. . . called to believe so that we can do even greater things
   than Jesus did (John 14:12)
. . . made into a dwelling place for the Trinity (John 14:23).

Those are not my words. They come from Jesus, and from
saints, who lived Jesus. I stand in awe. Do I dare believe such
things of myself? Can I embrace this call to splendor? The pages
of Scripture, the Word of God, are full of that call. The call is
persistent. We are called to be saints. Why not? Have you not
felt the stirring of the Divine deep within? Those three special
friends, C. S. Lewis, J. R. R. Tolkien, and Charles Williams,
joined together and formed a unique club called the Inklings,
because they had all had an inkling of the eternal. They had
had an inkling of something mysterious and wonderful moving
through the depths of their beings. They had had an inkling of
their greatness and splendor. Are you not perhaps an anonymous member of the Inklings? I am! I have an inkling of my
greatness. Of my littleness I have certitude. Yet the more I embrace the little one that I am, the more I have an inkling of
some mysterious greatness, something infinite stirring within
and yearning to be found. I feel it within me more each day. It
is like dynamite waiting to be ignited, like a treasure waiting to
be found, like a gift waiting to be given and received.

This is our story! It is a glorious story. We are little and
great. Both aspects must be embraced if we are to discover our
true selves. In owning our littleness we come to discover our
greatness. They are two gifts that become one when they are
understood and owned. A lack of understanding of these gifts
can lead only to frustration and denial of our true selves.

If we become preoccupied with our littleness, it can lead
only to discouragement. If we become preoccupied with our
greatness, it can lead only to disillusionment. Getting too absorbed in our littleness will cause us to despair. Getting too
absorbed in our greatness will cause those around us to despair.

It is possible to look at both our littleness and our greatness in ways that are healthy or in ways that are unhealthy. The difference between healthy and unhealthy is the difference between embracing and wallowing in. What we wallow in will make us sick; what we embrace will make us whole.

Even God became little. The All-Powerful One leaned down from heaven. The Indwelling One leaned out of our hearts. In that leaning God touched the earth. Heaven and earth became friends. It is no wonder, then, that we have an inkling of our greatness. It is no wonder that we have an inkling of another home, a place where peace and unity live full lives. It is no wonder we experience ourselves in process, on the way.

What is home but the merging of our lost selves? What is home but our divided selves finally embracing? Our house is abandoned no longer. We have entered, unafraid. We hear the murmur of a welcoming voice, "Come home, Little-Great-One, come home. Hansel and Gretel, come home. The birds have not eaten all the crumbs. Gather up the crumbs and come home."

A MAGNIFICAT FOR COMING HOME

O Most Creative One, ever bringing me to new life
O Most Powerful One, empowering me for life's journey
O Indwelling One, calling me to my Center
O Beloved One, loving me as I am.

Have you noticed that I'm coming home?
I have seen you, the All-Seeing One who sees me
I can remain away from home no longer
I just want to be there in you who are in me
for I have heard your call,
Make your home in Me
I can stay away from home no longer.

My soul proclaims the wonder of your friendship
My spirit is weeping within me for joy
My heart spills out tears with delight

They mix with my joy and I tremble
feeling totally claimed by your love.

You showed me that your home was within me
that living in me was your joy
I wept still more tears at the thought
of you in me and I in you,
A dwelling place I am, I kept saying
A home for the God of my life
My soul has turned into heaven
I am little and great all in one.

And then from within me, your voice came
giving me a name that was new
Little-Great-One, you called out, Come closer
Little-Great-One, Beloved, Come home
Come home to the self I keep loving
Come home to the truth that you are
Little-Great-One, you called out, Come closer
Little-Great-One, you kept saying, Come home.

You came with your all to my nothing
With such reverence you called out my name
You lifted me back into my poverty
the littleness I was trying to escape
Embracing that poverty, I felt wealthy
I was free at last to be great.

2. Frail and Glorious

The waters of baptism flowed over me
and no original sin was seen.
Rather, the Eye of God beheld
a tiny mass of bones and flesh
soul and spirit
infinite possibility
pure process
new, empty, and free,
free to choose
   good or evil
   light or darkness
   life or death
   grace or sin.

It was my original union
I was passing through the baptismal waters
being filled with power like unto God's
and God wept
at the possibility of *me*.

Then somewhere in between my baptism
   and my daily life
My power like unto God's became scattered
I forgot my original union with God.
And as I grew
I chose
   good and evil
   light and darkness
   life and death
   grace and sin.

With my baptism lost

I began to live my life fragmented,
standing on the edge of my baptismal powers
blind to their presence in the depths of my soul.

Yet all fragments are finally gathered up
and God does in us wonders
that others are not able to do.

So, on a day that felt like baptism
God gave me a glimpse of my hidden splendor,
made me aware of that original union
and my powers that had become scattered.
Now my life is ever spent
in calling home my scattered powers.

This poem was born out of a moment of anger. It happened like this. As I listened to the reading during our Evening Office I was suddenly jolted by a startling heresy. I could hardly believe what I was hearing. The reading was suggesting that a child, before baptism, was a tabernacle of the Devil. Tears came to my eyes and I wondered, how have we gotten things so backward? My anger turned into a holy sadness as this poem unfolded in my heart.

I certainly do not deny that we are born into a sinful condition, and at times I feel keenly we have inherited a mess. Still, I refuse to gaze at all this backward, seeing the sin first, as we have done in the past. Rather, I choose to see us as God beholds us: blessed, good, holy, noble, full of potential and exciting possibility—saints!

We have gotten so exclusively hung up on a Fall and Redemption theology that we tend to become obsessed with thoughts of our leanings toward evil. This is not to deny that we are sinners, but I am disheartened that we keep placing our original union with God and our infinite possibility for holiness in the background. I have come to believe that we fear our virtues far more than our sinfulness. We have inherited so much more than our sinful condition. It is certainly time to call back home the scattered powers of our baptism.

I have, at times, been called refreshingly heretical. I hope that means that I am not afraid to seek the truth, to explore unfamiliar lands, and to ask questions about things considered written in stone. It has been said that a heresy is just a truth pushed too far. My beginning reflection holds no heresy, but states a truth we are reluctant to ponder: the core of God within us. If it should ever happen that I push the truth entirely too far and find myself standing in the realm of heresy, may the eye of God and the wisdom of the Church help me sift out truth from falsehood.

One of the great lies of our day is that conversion is instant, like fast food. God can zap us and we're saved. It is all free. It costs nothing. Take it and run. This is what Bonhoeffer calls "cheap grace."[1] Punch in at church. Grab a sacrament and run. Season your conversation with "praise the Lord" and you're among the saved.

One of the great truths of our day is that conversion is on-going. Conversion is the process in which we are given opportunity upon opportunity to accept the free gift of salvation. Salvation is a free gift, yes, but it's costly. It's "costly grace." It costs us our lives lived passionately. The road to conversion is not a fast food line. When Saul was knocked down by that flash of lightning, that was not conversion. That was just God getting his attention. The conversion came as he groped his way in blindness to Ananias, able to see with interior eyes because he had no external eyes to depend on. His conversion continued day after day as he began to give meaning to his new name, Paul. He was still in the process of conversion when he was on his way to Rome in chains.

Yet there is no chaining the Word of God. Whether we believe that conversion is instant or ongoing, that Word will eventually get through to our hearts. God has such a yearning for our holiness to be rescued from the lies of this world that nothing will remain an obstacle forever unless we cling to it with such a tenacious grasp that we utterly refuse the divine embrace.

Conversion is what happens between birth and death. By putting emphasis on conversion as a process, I do not mean to disclaim the many accounts of people being suddenly and mysteriously touched by God and changed tremendously. There are too many stories of radical change in people's lives to take them lightly. However, even people who have had a dramatic encounter with the Divine, still must go through that daily purifying process of continued conversion. A deep and lasting conversion is a process, an unfolding, a slow turning and turning again.

We are saved every day. We are saved from our self-righteousness, our narrow minds, our own wills, our obstinate clinging. We are saved from our blindness. Salvation stands before us at every moment. It meets us face to face. It asks us to make a choice. Do we have the courage to accept it? It is costly, yet it brings life. The cross is always costly. It costs us our lives. The dust of our Lenten ashes turns before our very eyes into Easter glory. Our frailty fades into splendor. Our life given becomes life received and renewed.

Transformation! This is a wondrous, glorious truth. It is the Paschal Mystery. Life meets death. Death meets resurrection. This is our hope. We are frail and glorious creatures. Our frailty need not cripple us; our glory need not be denied. Embraced and cherished as part of the process that we are, these qualities become God's greatest advantage in our lives.

At birth, then, the eye of God beholds us as we really are, frail and glorious, little and great, weak and powerful. If Jesus wept over Jerusalem, meaning that he wept over the forgotten and lost potential of the people, why could he not also weep over the beauty and possibility of each human person at birth? I think he does. Our birth cry is a divine cry. It is God's cry meshed with our own, the holy scream of new life.

All too often in our early formation, our goodness and potential were downplayed; our sin and weakness were stressed in excess. The result is a world full of people who move through life without a felt sense of their basic goodness.

The most exciting of all calls is the call to be like God. The heart of our baptism and its deep meaning in our lives is an incorporation into the life of Christ. Saint Gregory of Nyssa, brother of Saint Macrina, said that if we want to know God we must strive to be like God. Our model for being like God is Jesus. Our baptism calls us to be like God in Christ.

There was a common belief in the Old Testament that if people were to see God face to face they would die. The reasoning behind this thought makes a great deal of sense. Our frailty simply can't take all of God's glory in one gaze. It would be too much for us. Our task, then, if we want to see God and live is to start looking like God. We must lessen the difference between us. A beautiful thought! This is our baptismal invitation, to be like God in Christ.

It is time, then, for us to embrace this frail flesh of ours with love. If we want to be disciples and saints, we must claim and cherish our humanness. What was good enough for God to embrace must be good enough for us. Let us try to take seriously the call to be divinized and stop hiding behind the mask of our frailty. There are hints of glory in our lives that yearn for fulfillment. The ache for God lives on in our depths. It gnaws at us and cries out to be named. If we walk back through our days, no doubt, we will come upon many frail and glorious moments—places where our poverty and our wealth touched each other. Three such moments have blessed me in particular: one from my life, one from the Scriptures, and one from a novel.

The first such moment that lingers in my memory was a moment of death. My seven-year-old sister died. I was only ten at the time. It was my first experience of death. We had had a quarrel before her death. There had not been opportunity for a reconciliation, and now she was gone. I sat underneath the big pine tree in our yard feeling very lost. There was nothing but frailty left. I wanted to console my parents, but I felt no joy. I only wanted to be left alone. Suddenly I felt an overwhelming love fill my entire being. It was a love that made me feel strong, noble, beautiful. I would not have used those words at the time, but reflecting back on the experience, they seem the most descriptive of that moment. That love flowed into a presence. It was as though I was not alone. Someone was with me. I was still sad, but a tremendous peace returned and I felt that life was too beautiful for any pain to totally crush me. I felt sad and strong. It was a frail and glorious moment.

The second frail and glorious moment came when I read Paul's letter to the Philippians (4:11–14) and heard him say:

I have learned to manage on whatever I have. I know how to be poor and I know how to be rich too. I have been through my initiation and now I am ready for anything anywhere: full stomach or empty stomach, poverty or plenty. There is nothing I cannot master with the help of the One who gives me strength.

How God must rejoice to dwell in a soul that has an attitude such as this! Here is the image of one who has embraced both frailty and glory. Let us pray for that grace.

The third frail and glorious moment that comes to mind is from Graham Greene's novel *The Power and the Glory*. The scene is that of a priest condemned to death during a religious persecution in Mexico. The tension in his life has driven him to depend too much on alcohol during his later years.

When he woke up it was dawn. . . . It was the morning of his death. He crouched on the floor with the empty brandy flask in his hand trying to remember an act of contrition. . . . He was confused . . . it was not the good death for which one always prayed. He caught sight of his own shadow on the cell wall. . . . What a fool he had been to think that he was strong enough to stay when others fled. What an impossible fellow I am, he thought. I have done nothing for anybody. I might just as well have never lived.

Tears poured down his face: he was not at that moment afraid of damnation. . . . He felt only an immense disappointment because he had to go to God empty-handed, with nothing at all. It seemed to him at that moment that it would have been quite easy to have been a saint. It would only have needed a little self-restraint and a little courage.

He felt like someone who had missed happiness by seconds at an appointed place. He knew now that at the end there was only one thing that counted—to be a saint.[2]

At this moment the whiskey-drinking priest can see nothing in his life except his frailty. His glory is hidden from him. You and I, stepping back from the story, can see so much more. His ache for God is obvious. He wanted to be a saint! Reading this story, it was easy for me to see his frailty and his glory, his littleness and his greatness.

The eye of God beholds so much more than we are able to see in our lives at any moment. Always our goodness and potential loom large under God's gaze. Why, then, is it so hidden from our sight? Are we not aware that when Paul says in his letters, "Give the saints greetings," he is talking about the saints on earth, not the saints in heaven? This is our vocation: *to be saints*. The journey to holiness begins this side of heaven. The taste of heaven begins right now. How hesitant we are to claim our inheritance!

We would think it strange to read about a person who died in poverty while having great material wealth stashed away somewhere within reach. Yet how often this is the truth of our spiritual lives! For as Father Plus, whom I referred to in my introduction to this book, has said, "In this frail envelope of our body is enclosed a great marvel."[3] We have riches that we refuse to own. Thomas Merton also makes loving reference to this marvel when he says:

Make ready for the Christ,
Whose smile,
like lightning,

Sets free the song of everlasting glory
That now sleeps,
in your paper flesh,
like dynamite.[4]

Our paper flesh is our frailty. The dynamite is our splendor. When the two meet, a song of everlasting glory will be born in our hearts. It will be the end of mediocrity in our lives and God will weep again, for joy.

Returning now to the poetic reflection that began this chapter, I ask you to turn your thoughts once more to baptism. The tragedy of baptism, at any age, is that so often we are incorporated into a Christian community that has forgotten its splendor. Frailty and dust are given predominance in teaching. The possibility of splendor, glory, and holiness, the call to be saints, is like wealth hidden away. As we celebrate baptism in the future, perhaps we can begin to see the face of Christ being etched on the one being baptized rather than original sin being washed away. Overemphasis on the magical wiping away of sin has created some very bad habits in church people. These bad habits emerge from an attitude that Bonhoeffer calls cheap grace.

Cheap grace is never truly valued because those receiving it put forth little effort on their own. The God of the person who is satisfied with cheap grace is a God who is always handing out rewards and fixing things up. The occupation of this God is to answer prayers.

Listen intently to the following questions. This is a brief examination of conscience. It can help you decide whether you are, at times, satisfied with cheap grace.

Why do parents rush into the church rectory wanting water poured over their children's heads, even though they are not participating members of a Christian community? Why do parents get upset when they are asked to attend a class on baptism before having their children baptized? Why do people become irate when the social justice gospel is preached from the altar? Why do we blame God for the suffering in the world? Why do we think that at the first sound of our cry for help, God should take away the addictions that we've spent years developing? Why does the baptism of a child during mass become a burden for people rather than a celebration?

In some way the answer to all these questions is that we've gotten used to the cheap grace of being uninvolved. We've gotten used to worshiping with hearts that aren't converted. Worship coming from an unconverted heart can only be empty ritual. If we are into empty ritual it is no wonder that we find a baptism during the eucharistic liturgy a bothersome burden adding little more than length to our Sunday worship.

The Israelite community was no different from our own. They, too, got used to the cheap grace of Yahweh throwing out manna to them. Like us, they forgot their part of the bargain. The covenant was two-sided: I will be your God *and* you will be my people. So often, like our fathers and mothers of ages past, we remember only one side of that covenant. *I will be your God* stays fresh in our memory. *You shall be my people* is too costly for us to take seriously, so we keep it at a distance. Yes, all too often we are content with the cheap grace of a soft, sweet religion that makes us feel good on the inside but bears no resemblance to the costly grace of the cross. Being God's people is costly. It costs us a little extra time on Sunday morning to welcome a new person into our faith community and let that baptism be a blessing rather than a burden. It costs us time to get involved.

In no way is it my intention to condemn people who seem to be satisfied with the cheap grace of having everything done for them and to them. The failure is not with the individual person, but with the total community. This is the system we've grown up in. We are not sufficiently aware of our connectedness to and our responsibility for one another. We do not fully appreciate the great honor it is to be brothers and sisters in the family of God.

Each time we choose cheap grace over costly grace, the baptismal waters dry up a bit more and we leave each other still further in the dust. Yet in God's great compassion, our splendor is rescued from the dust that settles on it. Through the dust we see the face of the risen Christ and our own face of glory. We are frail and glorious creatures. This is the gift of baptism. Our glory wins out. We become like God. The invitation of baptism is to be like God, which means being like Jesus. Two frail moments in the life of Jesus richly bless us: the crib and the cross. There was nothing obviously glorious about these two moments. His birth was in poverty. His death was also in poverty, outside the walls of Jerusalem, an outcast. These two frail moments became glorious. Our own frail moments can become glorious too.

Every time I say no to the birthing and dying that is set before me at the table of daily life, I seem to hear the echo of Jesus' words to the woman at the well, "If you but knew the gift of God . . ." Whether God weeps at the beauty and potential of our lives at birth or the lost potential of graced moments along the way, I hear that voice urging us to claim our splendor and our glory. "If you but knew the gift of God . . ."

The gift of God is the Divine Indwelling. It comes quietly into your frailty at baptism. You become a tabernacle for the Source of Life. When you come to understand this old yet often forgotten truth, you will know what is meant by the words *heaven on earth*. This is it! You are beginning to live heaven on earth in the Divine Indwelling. You, frail earth-creature, having given your frailty over to God, have created a place of splendor within the depths of your being, a holy and eternal space where you meet God face to face. Cherish this truth. It is costly grace.

> O frail and glorious creature
> whoever you are,
> Cherish this truth:
> > there are *hints of glory* in your being
> > *seeds of splendor*
> > *traces of holiness.*

> To be divinized is your destiny.

Your original union
yearns for a place in your life.

Walk gently, then, with your frailty
Allow it to bless you.
It will not cripple you
unless you run from it.
Embrace it instead.
Carry it as one carries
    the cherished secret of a great wealth
    hidden away in a holy, eternal space
    like a treasure hidden in a field.

That's you!
You fragile, noble being
Little-Great-One.
Yes, there are whispers of greatness
    in the frail envelope of your being.

The dust of the Ash Wednesdays of your life
    is tinged with the glory of your Easters.
Your tomb is a womb of life;
    you are hidden with Christ in God.
The dust of your life fades into glory.

O frail and glorious creature
from the crib to the cross
    to be divinized is your destiny.
Your original union cries out
    to become flesh in your life.
Your frailty and your glory
Your littleness and your greatness
    yearn to come home in your heart.

The heavens have heard
whispers of your splendor
and God still weeps at your birth.

3. Gather Up the Crumbs

We stand in the midst of nourishment and we starve. We dwell in the land of plenty, yet we persist in going hungry. Not only do we dwell in the land of plenty; we have the capacity to be filled with the utter fullness of God (Eph. 3:16–19). In the light of such possibility, what happens? Why do we drag our hearts? Lock up our souls? Why do we limp? Why do we straddle the issues? Why do we live so feebly, so dimly? Why aren't we saints?

Each of us could come up with individual answers to all these questions, but I want to suggest here a common cause. The reason we live life so dimly and with such divided hearts is that we have never really learned how to be present with quality to God, to self, to others, to experiences and events, to all created things. We have never learned to gather up the crumbs of whatever appears in our path at every moment. We meet all of these lovely gifts only half there. Presence is what we are all starving for. Real presence! We are too busy to be present, too blind to see the nourishment and salvation in the crumbs of life, the experiences of each moment. Yet the secret of daily life is this: *There are no leftovers!*

There is nothing—no thing, no person, no experience, no thought, no joy or pain—that cannot be harvested and used for nourishment on our journey to God.

What I am suggesting here is that everything in your life is a stepping-stone to holiness if only you recognize that you do have within you the grace to be present to each moment. Your presence is an energy that you can choose to give or not give. Every experience, every thought, every word, every person in your life is a part of a larger picture of your growth. That's why I call them crumbs. They are not the whole loaf, but they can be nourishing if you give them your real presence. Let everything energize you. Let everything bless you. Even your limping can bless you.

All too often we bemoan our imperfections rather than embrace them as part of the process in which we are brought to God. Cherished emptiness gives God space in which to work. We are pure capacity for God. Let us not, then, take our littleness lightly. It is a wonderful grace. It is a gift to receive. At the same time, let us not get trapped in the confines of our littleness, but keep pushing on to claim our greatness. Remind yourself often, "I am pure capacity for God; I can be *more*."

To help you discover in your own life just what those nourishing crumbs that call you back to your center might be, I am going to share with you some of the crumbs of my life. These are the experiences that are constantly calling out to me, asking that I allow them to bless and nourish me. The only way they can bless me is if I meet them face to face. That means I will need to give them my real presence. Although the experiences I mention here have indeed blessed me, there is a quality of presence and discipline still sadly lacking in my life, which accounts, I suppose, for the fact that I still live so half-heartedly. Yes, I blush at my mediocrity, for to be a member of a monastic community, a monk, for twenty-five years and still be so far from my center is, for sure, a scandal. On days when I am honest I see clearly the scandal and will not hide behind the lame excuse of my humanness. I have been called to be divinized. My baptism loudly announces that call. There is no such thing as an ordinary Christian. My baptism calls me, in Christ, to be like God. If we want to become like God, we cannot eat the whole loaf at once. It was never meant to be like that. We start small. We remember our littleness, our great need for nourishment. We remember, too, our call to greatness, our pure capacity for God. Yearning to be faithful to such a call, we reach out for every crumb in our path. We meet them face to face. We give them our real presence. We, so to speak, eat them.

Here are some of the experiences that have fed me and brought me to the heart of God. Gathering them up as crumbs means I do not receive them lightly. I do not treat them as leftovers, but as part of the whole loaf of God's plan for me. I feel honored and humbled for the opportunity of sharing these crumbs with you.

My love for trees.

There is something about a tree with its roots thrust deeply down into the nurturing earth, its trunk growing up to the heights, and its branches reaching out in all directions that has been, for me, a life symbol. Every time I meet a tree, if I am truly awake, I stand in awe before it. I listen to its voice, a silent sermon moving me to the depths, touching my heart, and stirring up within my soul a yearning to give my all.

There is one tree from my childhood that lives on in my memory as the most nurturing tree of all. Molly the Maple was my first chapel. She was the holy stairway I climbed to shelter myself from the storms of childhood. Her branches supported and protected me as I struggled with hurt feelings, misunderstandings, doubts, angers, growing up. Her leafy sanctuary hid me from pursuing brothers and sisters and other unwanted intruders. Her arms held me as I wondered about life, as I cried and prayed and asked God questions that are only now beginning to be answered.

Trees are still sanctuaries for me, holy places where I can rest. I climb them less often today, but I still find as I lean my head against a tree that voices from within are calling my name.

Moments of beauty.

What is unique about a moment that has the power to bless us and the potential to feed us is not so much the power of the moment itself, but rather the quality of presence we bring to that moment. Our presence can change an ordinary, unnoticed moment into a moment of beauty that can feed the soul. The awareness, the goodness and depth of you and me come face to face with the reality, the goodness and depth of another person, an event, a place or thing. In this meeting is born a moment of beauty, a celebration, but for this to happen, we've got to be there with quality. It isn't so much that the moment isn't beautiful without us. Rather, the moment cannot bless us without us. We've got to be there with our souls, not just our bodies. It is the difference between being alive or dead to something.

Moments of beauty! They are everywhere. They are every day. You've seen them. You've been in the heart of them. Magnificent as they may seem at the time, they are only crumbs, pieces of the whole loaf. Let's walk back through the pages of our hearts and remember some of these moments:

. . . snowflakes falling so fast that the sky was suddenly full of angels

. . . a physical therapist working reverently with a person who is learning to walk again after a car accident

. . . a bud on a Christmas cactus that you thought was dead

. . . a sunset that is so breathtakingly beautiful you stop the car to just be with it

. . . the steam from your early morning coffee or tea slowly ascending, meeting the first rays of dawn

. . . an old face aglow because of your unexpected visit

Those moments seem naturally beautiful, yet it might surprise you how often you miss such moments completely. If you walk back through your day each evening, you may be close enough to some of those missed moments that you can still capture a bit of the blessing that was meant to be yours.

One special moment of beauty that stands out in my mind I experienced in a bus station. Taking my head out of my book for a moment proved to be true nourishment. I witnessed a little girl helping her brother get a drink at the water fountain. Attempting to lift him to the proper height turned out to be impossible. I was just at the point of giving them some assistance when quick as lightning she darted over to a shoeshine man, pointed to a footstool he wasn't using, dragged it to the water fountain, and very gently lifted up her thirsty brother. It all happened so fast and it was so simple, yet it turned out to be a moment of beauty that became a prayer for me. So much to be learned from such a little moment. Perhaps what touched me most was her readiness to seek out a way to take care of the need without waiting to be rescued. It was a moment of beauty: a small child with a single heart.

Sin and weakness in my life.

There is nothing like felt inadequacy to help me depend solely on God. What is sin but not living up to your potential, not being all that God calls you to be? You are pure capacity for God. Your emptiness accepted creates a space for God in your life. When you embrace that emptiness, God can begin to fill you. God has a plan for you. Sin is living according to your own plan. Sin is trying to fill up your own life rather than allowing God to fill you. Sin is being willing to stay where you are rather than go through the pain and joy of being in process. Saint Basil the Great said that sin is not using the power for good that God placed within you.

Feeling in your guts your powerlessness without God is an important part of coming to union with God. Nothing can so enable you to feel your own powerlessness as to finally be able to own your sin and embrace it as Jesus did on the cross. Jesus embraced our sin, took it to himself, and said, "You are not guilty." Until you and I embrace our sin, take it to ourselves on our own crosses, we will never feel free even though Jesus has freed us. We will remain feeling guilty. If you are into gathering up crumbs, gather up your sins and let them save you. Take your sin. Feel it. Look at yourself and say, "Yes, this is me trying to live according to my own plan, and yet loved by God just the way I am."

I want to tell you a story about my first sin. This was the first time I can recall turning away from my potential and following my own plan instead of God's plan. I must have been about eight years old. Mom and Dad had taken me shopping. They gave me a dime and told me it was mine to spend in any way I wished. We were very poor. A dime was like a dollar to me. Like all kids, I loved candy. I can still see myself stopping at the candy counter and choosing a candy bar called DIP, bold yellow letters on a red background. It just cost a nickel, so I would have one nickel left to save. As I stood by the cash register waiting my turn, my face fell upon the old man and woman in the line in front of me. They were counting pennies as though they didn't have quite enough money to pay for their groceries. It seems they were just five or six cents short. They picked up a package of morning glory seeds to put back on the shelf. Then I heard God's call. It was loud. It was clear. Into my child's heart it came, "Put back your candy; give them the dime." I struggled inwardly but I couldn't do it. I couldn't love them enough to let them keep their morning glories. I kept my candy and my nickel instead. I left the store sad. The candy did not make me happy that day. I could not explain my tears to my parents in spite of their questions. I never forgot that incident. It taught me more about what sin is than any teachers have ever taught me. What I remember most about that experience is that I never confessed it because I thought the priest wouldn't understand that it was a sin. I thought I had to make up something that really sounded *bad*. Deep inside I understood sin in a way that I couldn't explain to adults. The wisdom I had as an eight-year-old child on that day could only have come from God. I have embraced that sin all these years. It never made me feel bad; sad, lonely, and beautiful, yes—but not bad. Many grown-ups still do not understand sin.

Being able to recognize and admit that I am wrong.

This isn't an easy crumb, but it's so freeing. It is such a burden to always need to be right. I remember with some amusement my difficulty in being wrong as a child. If anyone told me that something was wrong, like my shoe was untied or a button was in the wrong buttonhole, I would simply say, "I like it like that," Then when no one was looking I would set things right.

The things that are sometimes wrong in my life have gone far beyond untied shoes and unbuttoned buttons, but the memory of my insistent "I like it like that" lingers with me and makes me smile. I have come to realize that, no, I don't like it like that! I don't like that stubborn streak in me that insists on being right. Needing to be right all the time comes out of my insecurity. As I mature, that need to be right diminishes.

Mistakes can be such friends. They rough up my smooth edges, convincing me that I don't have to be perfect to be loved. What a freedom to be able to say, "I was wrong"! What's wrong with being wrong? Now more than ever I can truly say, "I like it like that." It is such a burden to have to be right all the time.

Loneliness.

Except for my lonely moments, I think I could quite easily forget that I am not a separate existence apart from God. My loneliness attracts me to the feet of Jesus. Like a magnet I am drawn there, longing to be all one with God. The separateness I keep choosing makes me desperately homesick, and so I am willing, at last, to surrender my divided heart. I am homesick to be one with God. Union with God is the only heaven there is, and it begins here on earth. Jesus said that there was a baptism he had to undergo, and he felt extreme anguish until it was accomplished. I know the feeling, Jesus. I feel the anguish, too. There is someone I must become. There is someone I must be grafted onto, and how lonely I am until it is accomplished!

My loneliness blesses me because it shows me that I'm not enough all by myself, and so I am impelled to reach out my arms and heart to God and to others. My loneliness blesses me because it encourages me to allow myself to be vulnerable. My loneliness blesses me because it won't let me hide in the illusion of my self-sufficiency.

If you're hungry for growth, spend time with your loneliness.

People.

You may be thinking, "Well, for sure, some people are pretty crummy," but I was going to suggest that each person you meet is more like a loaf of uncut fresh bread. It is difficult to fathom the depth and potential of each person you meet. This depth and potential are like treasures hidden in a field. The field is that surface self that shows at first glance, but oh, the resources to be found within! Each person is a lot like you, deep and not yet fully explored, scared and beautiful, fragile and strong. People are nourishing. When your depth meets the depth of another person, what a sacrament that can be! Sometimes it's the birth of a lasting relationship, sometimes just a deep insight, but nourishing all the same.

Because most of us meet quite a few people during our lifetimes, I want these words to be an encouragement to you to linger awhile over each person you meet, each person you live with, each relationship, even those people you see walking through the crowds, the strangers you do not know. Look on them with love. Contemplate them. Take them into your heart.

It is easy to miss the very people you live with. It is easy to get so used to them that you start taking them for granted. It is easy for the moments spent together to go by and remain moments untouched and unblessed. We can end up treating members of our own household like strangers even though we are standing side by side and sitting down to eat at the same table.

It is possible to take our closest relationships and our best friends for granted. The heart cannot live without intimacy. We all need special people in our lives to whom we can show our souls. But relationships need to be nurtured, nourished, and celebrated. Friendship won't last without food. How do you feed your friendships?

There are also the crowds of people—yes, even the crowds. Next time you walk through a crowd at the shopping center or on the street, try to see the people as individuals. They are people who share the earth with you. They are the Body of Christ. You have a common God. Your pathways may be different, but the love God has for each is the same.

Bless them, then, by seeing them. Look on them with love. If Jesus' look was enough to bless and heal others, yours can be, too. So when you are out on the highway and you dim your lights for them, pray for them. Let your light-dimming become a gift of love, a sacrament, a meeting. A moment saved, saved because you were there.

Criticism.

Sometimes the most unlikely things can nourish us. I am certainly not one who loves criticism, but reflecting on the many things that have blessed me, I would have to include this uncomfortable little guest. I call it a guest because always when I am criticized that word of criticism, welcome or unwelcome, moves in on me, sets up a tent in my heart, looks me square in the eye, and says, "Well, what do you think? True or false?" What I think is that many times the criticism is right on target, something I needed to hear. I have come to understand that when someone criticizes me, even when the criticism is not given in love, I can learn from it. The choice is mine. I can sit in self-pity, licking my wound, or I can ask myself, "Well, what about it? Is there any truth in this?" Sometimes there is much truth in the criticism. Sometimes if I look deep enough, I find just a little truth, so little that it could have been missed had I not taken it to prayer. Sometimes there seems to be no truth in it at all. If that is the case, then I try to forget it and go on with the wonderful gift of life.

I write about this because it is so close to my heart. In my lifetime I have had people say really critical things to me, not said in love at all. In my earlier years I completely missed the things that were said to me in anger, and could barely look at the things that were said in love. Now I see more clearly how God can use sinful, imperfect people to teach me. Why should I refuse to learn just because the gift comes in a package not so nicely wrapped? Sometimes I learn more about myself from my enemies than from my friends. I do not use *enemies* here in the harsh sense of someone who literally hates me, but rather someone who doesn't exactly dote on me.

Who do I think I am that I can never be criticized unjustly? I who follow a crucified Savior ought to be able to embrace even false criticism as gift and go on joyfully with life. The freeing thing is to be able to have the humility to look at myself with loving, microscopic eyes and then go on from there. This is all a part of my potential to let everything nourish me.

Sitting at someone's feet.

At someone's feet has not been my favorite place to hang out. As I grow older, however, I have such a yearning to sit at the feet of one who is wise. I long for wisdom, and I've discovered that I can't get wisdom from books. Wisdom comes from listening to life. If you find someone who has lived life fully and is still full of life, you have found a treasure. Learn from him or her. Lean on her heart as John leaned on Jesus at the Last Supper. Sit at his feet as Mary sat at the feet of Jesus. It is not only at the table that we find nourishment. Sometimes the food we need is found in lowly places. Until we learn to sit at one another's feet, we will starve at our lavish banquet tables.

Sorrow.

There's nothing like sorrow to get your attention. It is almost as though sorrow pulls presence out of you. In the midst of sorrow there's nothing to do but be there and celebrate the hurt. We celebrate the hurt through holy screams. Holy screams come from the heart. They are screams that people often, in their ignorance, try to smother. Don't let them take your screams away too early. Holy resignation comes only after holy screams. Don't let them tell you it's God's will, unless they are saying that life is God's will and freedom is God's will, and *you* are God's will. Much of the news you see on television each evening is not God's will. It is the will of the human race. It is too comfortable to blame it on God. Why blame the One who wills nothing for you except that you be divinized?

Ask yourself only one question when you are in sorrow: Am I being divinized? Am I becoming like God? Then listen to the holy scream of Jesus on the cross, "My God, my God, why have you forsaken me?" Only then did Jesus bow his head in holy resignation.

If you have never thanked people for suffering for you, I invite you to begin. And if you cannot thank them out loud, then pray silently before them, "We adore you O Christ and we bless you, because by your sufferings you are redeeming the world."

We are absent from life far too much. Sorrow makes it impossible for us to be absent, and so, blesses us with real presence. In the midst of our sorrows, distractions fall away, and we are there, raw and open, often confused, always vulnerable, little and great. In sorrow we are nudged to our depths. I do not claim to understand the mystery of suffering, but I often meet people who have walked through great sorrow; they seem to wear the face of God. These are the people at whose feet I yearn to sit.

Fasting.

Fasting makes me vulnerable and reminds me of my frailty. It leads me to remember that if I am not fed I will die. Fasting nourishes me and gets me in touch with a deeper hunger. All deep hungers nourish me. I am nourished because I am brought to a place where I can live in denial no longer.

Standing before God hungry, I suddenly know who I am. I am one who is poor, called to be rich in a way that the world does not understand. I am one who is empty, called to be filled with the fullness of God. I am one who is hungry, called to taste all the goodness that can be mine in Christ. Standing before God hungry helps me know deeply my own need. Most of us have to taste our need in a fierce sort of way before our hungers jar us into turning our lives over to God.

Fasting is cleansing. It cleans out our bodies. It lays bare our souls. It leads us into the arms of that One for whom we hunger. In the Divine Arms we become less demanding and more like the One who holds us. Then we experience new hungers. We hunger and thirst for justice, for goodness and holiness. We hunger for what is right. We hunger to be saints.

Most of us are not nearly hungry enough for the things that really matter. That's why it is so good for us to feel a gnawing in our guts. Then we remember why we are fasting. We remember all the peoples of the world who have no choice but to go to bed hungry. We remember how we waste and squander the goods of this world. We remember what poor stewards of the earth we have been. We remember that each of us is called to be bread for the world. Our lives are meant to nourish. Fasting can lead us to the core of our being and make us more nourishing for others.

Words.

I love words. How full of power they are! What a source of healing, consolation and joy, hope and encouragement they can be for others! People can die for lack of words. They can starve just longing for a human voice. A word of kindness is a Word made Flesh! Think of the words that have been spoken, written, and sung throughout the ages. The human story is continually told through the great works of literature, history, psychology, science, and so on. Our response to all words, if we want them to feed us, is to listen and connect them to our lives.

Not all words are nourishing. Words can also intimidate and stifle growth. These words are destructive. They wound rather than heal; they discourage rather than encourage. It is both frightening and awesome to be aware of how much power we have. Power to bless! Power to curse! Let us get on, then, with the task of blessing, as we remember in the words of Isaiah our power to use our words for good: "The Lord God has given me a well trained tongue that I might know how to speak to the weary a word that will rouse them. Morning after morning he opens my ear that I may hear . . ." (Isa. 50:4 NAB).

Silence.

The secret of this well-trained tongue is found not in speaking, but in silence. If you want your words to be powerful words of blessing, words that nourish others, then learn to be silent. The world is afraid of silence. Radios blare. Televisions are never turned off. The stereo is on at top volume. The voice speaks whether or not it has something to say.

A sign on my calendar reads, "Don't talk unless you can improve on silence." I swallow hard. These words convict me as I reflect on the many times I chatter on with words that do not nourish. Silence gently draws us to our depth. By letting go of our many words we are drawn to that One Word made Flesh, that Word that gives life and power to all of our spoken words.

I love silence. I love words. Silence and words have been at war within my soul for as long as I can remember. Unfortunately, all too often I have chosen words over silence. Silence is scarey. It is frightening to be so utterly with yourself. Then, too, the world affirms me more for my words than for my silence. How could the world affirm what it does not understand? But we, whom Jesus said are not of this world, surely we can come to understand silence and feel at home in its embrace.

In my community we have returned to the practice of Grand Silence beginning at 9:00 p.m. and continuing until after breakfast the next morning. To be silent alone is one thing, but I have come to love being silent together. To give up words as a community is to attempt to go to the depths together. At breakfast I feel as though we are all waiting together for God's saving touch. There are so many ways we are still unsaved. "It is good to wait in silence for Yahweh to save" (Lam. 3:26).

Prayer.

This list of crumbs to be gathered up for nourishment could continue on through the night and into the new day. There is no better way to end this chapter than by reflecting with you on that golden response to God called prayer.

To pray is to touch God and let God touch us. It is a matter of presence and response. Prayer does nothing to make God more present, for God is always present. Prayer is our response to the presence of God in our lives. A friend comes to see us. What do we do? We reach out to touch and receive that friend. We allow this friend, in some way, to touch us. Friendship is a marvelous exchange, and that is exactly what prayer is.

So how do I pray? I listen. I talk. I weep. I am silent. I embrace the beloved. I gaze with reverence. I wonder and adore. I share my needs. I have tea with God. I give gifts. I receive gifts. I give thanks and I say I'm sorry. I scream. I get angry. I show God all my life, including my very divided heart. I relax. I'm at home. Sometimes I read a poem or tell God a story. Sometimes I dance. God loves stories and poems and dances. Sometimes I get a bit dramatic with God. What do I say to God? What words do I use when I do use words? I say:

O Most Powerful One, O Indwelling One, I have no words to bring you into my heart; for already you have emptied yourself into my life. You came uninvited. You are here. But I am afraid to reach out and touch you. I am afraid of falling in love. Don't you see that if I fall in love I will have to surrender to your embrace. I will have to let you love me as I am, with all my imperfections. I will have to give you my will. O God, I love my own will! I am not ready to give it up. I stand at this east window each morning yearning for you. I yearn for you just as the sun yearns to rise. My soul, too, has sunrises, but they aren't seen by the world yet. I keep my rising inside. In spite of my struggle to keep it inside, I almost burst with you, God, each day. What would the world think if I rose? If I rose I could never be my shallow, surface self anymore. If I rose some people would not like my colors, and so I keep all this lovely color inside. I am afraid to rise. O-Beloved-One, I am dying of yearning to rise. I am dying to come home to myself. It is the same as coming home to you. O All-Seeing-One, can you see that this yearning is pure prayer? Can you see that my yearning is a golden sunrise?

My fear suddenly falls away. God recognizes the cry of my heart as prayer. I feel the recognition and though I thought it was God's recognition, it was really my own. There is no doubt about it. Prayer is a marvelous exchange.

> I stand at my window and watch
> one by one the stars all leave me
> I am having tea with the dawn
> the first ray of sun descending
> into my teacup
> into my heart
> The steam of my tea ascending
> to the heavens
> into God's heart
> The yearning in my heart streaming
> to the heavens
> into God's heart
> And God, standing in the heavens
> watching the sun rise in my heart
> leans down to breathe in
> the first rays of my yearning
> and names it *morning prayer*.
> What a marvelous exchange!

Prayer! The golden necessity! The glorious crumb! The cry of all cries! What is my cry among all the cries of the world?

Only a crumb, but a crumb that nourishes the heart of God. God needs our cries. God has to love, and who is there to love if not me, if not you?

We will continue our reflections with a woman who came crying after God, a woman who understood the value of crumbs. With her insight and single heart to lead us on, let us starve no more.

4. The Prayer of a Woman Who Understood Crumbs

Matthew and Mark share with us a story in the Gospels about a woman who was willing to settle for crumbs.[1] Now this willingness may not seem so spectacular, but in a world such as ours where everyone wants the biggest and the best, it does seem a bit unusual to meet someone who is willing to be saved, healed, and fed just with crumbs.

The woman's daughter had a demon. What kind of demon I really don't know, but we are all acquainted with demons, aren't we? Sometimes they are more subtle than the Devil in person. They are those things that clutch at us, strangle us, force us to obey them. They control us with great delight, and finally they own us. Demons are certainly as much around today as they were in Jesus' day. They are more subtle, perhaps, and so we think we have outgrown them. Because we call them by other names, we have a way of missing them. But there is still a great force surrounding us that tries to push us into what is not of God. Watch out for these demons. If a friend, a daughter or son, a sister or brother of yours has a demon, or if the demon is your own, by all means go to the Lord. Insist that the demon be cast out.

We return to our story, then. The woman had no name. She could be you or me. And her daughter, too, could be any one of us. Although the woman wasn't one of the chosen ones—in her day she was called a Gentile dog—she came crying after Jesus, "Have mercy on me, Lord, Son of David, my daughter is severely possessed by a demon." She called him Lord. What the members of the household had failed to acknowledge, a pagan, outcast woman proclaimed loudly: "O Lord, my daughter is severely possessed by a demon."

It was a dilemma. Jesus did have a problem. How do you respond when a Gentile cries for mercy? He answered her not a word.

What do you do when Jesus answers you not a word? When the silence of God happens to me—and it does more often than I'm comfortable with—there are a number of temptations I struggle with. There is the temptation to self-pity. I begin to feel sorry for myself because I've asked God for a significant favor and it is as though I am speaking into a vacuum. Here I am in a moment of need and God hangs that great silence on me. It is discouraging, and so I begin to sit in self-pity. It is not a pleasant place to be.

The second temptation is the temptation to let my joy slip away. I allow God's silence and seeming disinterest to make me sad. Sometimes I am angry. This is a temptation I try hard to overcome, because I am basically a joyful person, and it seems unfair to the people I live and work with to take my joy away from them because I am having a problem with God.

My third temptation is the temptation to just go away. God hasn't answered my plea, so I don't ask again. I ignore the One who is ignoring me. I look at God's silence as rejection. I refuse to risk a second rejection, so I just go away. I hear the disciples saying, "Send her away," so I go before anyone has a chance to send me. Yes, this is the great temptation: to go away! To walk away when things are difficult! This is the temptation not to hang in there with the pain, the questions, the uncertainty and confusion. It is the temptation not to wait for the dawn to come.

But our woman? What did she do with Jesus' blank stare? He answered her not a word. When his silence finally ended, the word that came definitely was not the word of life that she was yearning for. After that embarrassing silence with his disciples begging him to send her away, Jesus told her that he had been sent only to the lost sheep of Israel. And what was her response, this rejected Gentile woman? She did a marvelous act and one we could all learn from. Her response was what we call faith. She came and knelt before him, saying, "Lord, help me!"

Her response gives me hope. I love it. There are some of us who have forgotten how to kneel, and I am one of those with that poor memory. Yet when there is nothing left to do and nowhere else to go, it is then I remember my knees. I remember my frailty. When you're little and poor and you've no place to go, being on your knees before Jesus isn't a bad choice at all.

So there she was, that visionary, loving, bold woman, on her knees before Jesus, calling him Lord, crying out "Help me!" The words he finally gave to her sounded like anything but help. His silence had been less insulting. "It's not fair," Jesus told her, "to take the children's bread and throw it to the dogs." Her answer was quick: "Yes, Lord, even the dogs eat the crumbs that fall from the master's table."

I am in awe of this woman's persistence, humility, and vision. She simply wouldn't take no for an answer. Put-downs didn't seem to faze her. And why was that? It was because her heart was undivided. She knew what she wanted. She had come to Jesus seeking help for someone she loved. She would not allow her own hurt feelings to stand in the way of her prayer for help. She believed he was Lord! He called her a dog and she reminded him that the dogs get the crumbs that fall from the table.

I love all that spirit in her, her love for her daughter, her boldness, her belief in Jesus, that beautiful persistence, her willingness to challenge Jesus, her lack of self-pity, her humility and faith. All of this I find attractive, but there are two things in this woman that stand out as awesome. They are the two qualities I most desire. First, I long for her undivided heart, a heart that is so single it knows what it wants—in this case, healing for her daughter. When your thoughts are turned radically toward someone else, you don't have time to feel sorry for yourself. Second, I am touched by her vision. It is a vision that recognizes nourishment even in the crumbs. Crumbs are little things, a little portion of something much larger. Crumbs are insignificant. Crumbs are what most people overlook, even in the spiritual life, because they are so busy grabbing for the whole loaf. But this woman didn't overlook them. Her heart was too single and pure to miss even the opportunity of a crumb. Someone she loved was in need. She would not be put off even by the Lord of all the earth. And so she said, "OK, you're saving the loaf for your family? I know I'm outside the household—a dog, you called me. Well, even the dogs get the crumbs that fall from the table. If you're saving the loaves for your children, I'll settle for the crumbs." It was as though she were saying, "Look, I don't need a lot, not a big, flashy, head-line healing! Just a crumb! Just a word! Just a look of love! Just desire my daughter's healing! That will be enough."

And Jesus? Jesus was impressed. Her deep faith had touched his heart. He let her in. He forgot about tradition for the moment. He saw only a person in love and a person in need. Can you allow it to matter who the law says you've come for, when you're standing face to face with someone that much in love and that much in need? Jesus put the law aside and centered on the person before him. "O woman," he said, "great is your faith. Be it done for you as you desire." And her daughter was healed instantly.

Jesus saw the poverty within her that she had already embraced. Her actions show us that she was living out of that poverty of spirit. She didn't deny her littleness, but neither did she wallow in it. She embraced it. Even in her kneeling, she stood tall. She was her self, her best self.

Jesus saw a greatness in this woman that most likely even she didn't recognize. He looked at her with love and said, "Lit-tle-Great-One, come home! Even if you aren't part of the family by law, through love you are, so *come home*." Because this wom-an embraced her littleness and didn't let it stifle and cripple her, this story, her story, will be told down through the ages.

What a wonderful story! It can be your story! Has it ever occurred to you that Jesus might be impressed with your faith, your hope, your love? Has it ever occurred to you that because of your single, pure, undivided heart, Jesus might look at you with love and say, "I like what I see. Your faith nourishes me. I can do nothing but respond to your great need. Be it done for you as you desire"?

The reason the story of this gospel woman touches me so much is that she is me. I know what it's like to stand before the Lord in need, asking for grace and light, for bread and understanding. I know what it's like to get no answer, to have God hang that great silence on me.

I know what it feels like to want God like I want my own breath. I know what it feels like to experience nothing but darkness and silence. I am numb with my nothingness. I am angry at God for not coming. I have little tolerance for an absent God. God has never come quickly in my life except for those moments when I wasn't waiting, those unexpected gifts of grace rained down from heaven as pure gift. During such moments I change my mind about my anger toward God, just the way God did about his anger toward us in the Old Testament. I relent and forgive God for the long night of darkness, the terrible deafening silence.

It is my hope that has saved me most. I have a lucky disposition. I am not able to despair. This has been my salvation. No matter how faint the glimmer of light, or how small the crumb of bread, there is something within me that won't allow me to give up on God or myself or others. It feels like a loving anger, an intense passion that drives me to be angry enough to wait and insist but not so angry that I get bitter. Personally, I think it is a monastic anger, a moderate, balanced anger. About this anger, I can only say, it feels healthy.

For when I am so angry at God for not coming, yet so hungry for God's presence, some kind of miracle always happens in my life. Sometimes it's the miracle of finding myself on my knees and hearing the voice of the Beloved saying, "Be it done for you as you desire."

GATHER UP THE CRUMBS AND LIVE

O Most-Nourishing-One, if I asked you for bread,
   would you hand me a stone?
I'd believe in the stone,
   if it came from you!

Oh, God, where is the bread?
I've sat with open hands for hours.
Is my heart as open as my hands?
Or is this just an empty symbol,
   devoid of meaning
   devoid of reality?
Is my closed heart laughing at my open hands?

I hear the songs they sing in churches:
You satisfy the hungry with gift of finest wheat . . .
And I wonder, where is this gift of finest wheat?
Have I become the Canaanite woman to you, Lord?
Are you afraid to throw your bread to dogs,
   to the unworthy
   the blind
   the outsiders?
Well then, I'll put on her mind instead of yours.
I'll wear her faith instead of your arrogance.
Even the dogs get the crumbs, Lord.

God, you cannot hide from me.
You cannot scare me with your face of absence.
I scare myself with this hunger for your presence.
I would break all rules to possess you.
To be nourished by you,
   I would go to every table in the world.
I would leave no stone unturned to find you
   lest when I turn it over
   it be changed to bread.
I come looking for bread,

but if you're saving it for your children,
   don't worry.
I'll gather up the crumbs if you insist.
I'll make a meal on leftovers
   and rejoice that I have been so blessed.

O Most-Powerful-One
I feel so powerless
   so little and so poor
   so vulnerable
   so terribly wide open
   so seen.
It hurts to be so hungry
   so dependent on your bits of grace.

Even the dogs get the crumbs, Lord
I'll gather up the crumbs
   and live.

5. Into the Eye of God

For your prayer
  your journey into God,
may you be given a small storm
  a little hurricane
  named after you,
persistent enough
  to get your attention
violent enough
  to awaken you to new depths
strong enough
  to shake you to the roots
majestic enough
  to remind you of your origin:
    made of the earth
    yet steeped in eternity
    frail human dust
    yet soaked with infinity.

You begin your storm
  under the Eye of God.
A watchful, caring eye
  gazes in your direction
  as you wrestle
  with the life force within.

In the midst of these holy winds
In the midst of this divine wrestling
  your storm journey
  like all hurricanes
  leads you into the eye,
Into the Eye of God
  where all is calm and quiet.

> A stillness beyond imagining!
> Into the Eye of God
>   after the storm
> Into the silent, beautiful darkness
> Into the Eye of God.

All living things have a heart. I have come to the heart of this book. This chapter is the link between the first four chapters and the last four because it is here that I offer you a way of gathering up the crumbs, a way of prayer that, for me, is pure gold. Here is a way to harvest the Word of God.

The monastic tradition to which I belong has always stressed the value of seeking intimate communion through persistent dwelling with and in the Word of God. We call this form of prayer Lectio Divina (Divine Reading). Lectio Divina is far more than what we ordinarily understand as spiritual reading. It is reading with the divine, inner eye. It is reading with the eye of God, under the eye of God. It is reading with the desire to be totally transformed by the Word of God, rather than just to acquire facts about God.

The incarnational aspect of Christianity reminds us that all of life is full of God. God is in all. Lectio Divina, then, is a way of reading God in everything. Under the eye of God, we read God everywhere, until finally we move into the eye of God.

In the tradition of our desert fathers and mothers and early monastic communities from which the practice of Lectio Divina slowly emerged, the emphasis was on the reading of the Scriptures. This was the Word of God par excellence. The disciple was encouraged to hover over the Word of God in the Scriptures as the Spirit once hovered over the birthing world. In the midst of this hovering the disciple is born from above. The one who is immersed in the Word of God in the Scriptures is eventually able to read God in all things. Divine Reading becomes a way of life. With our inner, divine eye we read God in the poets, the saints, the philosophers, the earth, in our experiences, in everything. The table of daily life becomes a banquet to which we are always invited.

It was the ascetics of the Middle Ages who began to develop Lectio Divina as a process leading to inner prayer. I refer especially to the monk Guigo II, a twelfth-century Carthusian. In a delightful letter on the contemplative life called *The Ladder of Monks*, Guigo divides the experience of Lectio into four phases or degrees: reading, meditation, prayer, contemplation (*lectio, meditatio, oratio, contemplatio*).[1]

Reading, he says, puts food whole into the mouth. Meditation chews it, digs for the treasure. Prayer extracts the flavor and helps us to get to know the treasure. Contemplation embraces and welcomes the thirsty soul. In contemplation nothing is left except being in God. The first three degrees work so beautifully together that it is difficult to tell where one degree begins and the other ends. It is all part of one process leading to contemplative union with God.

I could go into more detail about the wisdom I have gained from other spiritual seekers who have practiced Lectio Divina, but because I want to stress the importance of trusting one's own experience in prayer rather than modeling one's life after experts, I choose to focus these reflections on my own experience of Divine Reading. My beginning advice to you is this: Always read the Scriptures with a heart ready to repent. Receive the storm that repentance brings. Let the holy winds toss you to and fro. You will be awakened to new depths as you wrestle with the life forces within. What seems like violence at first will lead you gently into the eye of God where all is calm and quiet, like the eye of a hurricane. When you finally surrender and stop fighting the winds, you will be carried by angels into the eye of God. There, you will rest in peace and learn to see like God. It will be the great harvest of contemplation— through the storm into the quiet.

There is a quote from Benedictine Abbot Marmion that has become a guide for me as I spend time in Divine Reading each day. He says,

> Read under the eye of God
> until your heart is touched,
> then give yourself up to love.[2]

I see these instructions as corresponding with Guigo's four degrees. Let us consider each in turn, plus a fifth degree of my own.

1. *Read under the eye of God (Guigo's reading phase).*

This is a special and unique way of reading. It is a slow, reflective reading, reading with a longing to be touched, healed, and transformed by the Word. It is not at all, then, a hurried reading. It is quality reading rather than quantity. Just as when you sit down at the dinner table, you do not necessarily eat everything on the table, so too, when you approach the table of the Scriptures, you are not there to cover territory.

Nutritionists tell us that to get full benefit from the food we eat, we should chew slowly. In other words, eat contemplatively. The same is true of the food of the Scriptures. To be fully nourished by the richness hidden in these words you must hover over them slowly and reverently as one who is certain of finding a treasure. Your search for the treasure, though, is not a desperate, hurried, frantic search. Rather, you search calmly and with assurance. You will find the treasure. You will be fed. You will be transformed.

Remembering that we are reading under the eye of God is an immense help for our distracted hearts. We are naturally distracted creatures. We do not yet own the undivided hearts we yearn for. Remembering that we are reading under the eye of God can help us remain open to the possibility of that divine eye guiding us in our reading. If we accept the loving gaze of that eye, it will indeed hover over us as we read. It will penetrate us, heal us, and open our eyes to the truth. It will embrace us. It will look down upon us. It will look out from within us. It will read through us and we will be changed by its unfailing gaze in our direction.

We do not always realize what a radical suggestion it is for us to read to be formed and transformed rather than to gather information. We are information seekers. We love to cover territory. It is not easy for us to stop reading when the heart is touched; we are a people who like to get finished. Lectio offers us a new way to read. Read with a vulnerable heart. Expect to be blessed in the reading. Read as one awake, one waiting for the beloved. Read with reverence.

We are naturally reverent beings, but much of our natural reverence has been torn away from us because we have been born into a world that hurries. There is no time to be reverent with the earth or with each other. We are all hurrying into progress. And for all our hurrying we lose sight of our true nature a little more each day. This is precisely why we need to believe in the eye of God hovering over us. We are not alone. There is One with us who wants to give us back our reverence. There is One with us who wants to give us back the gift of time.

Read the Scriptures, then, with reverence, giving up the lie that you don't have time. Read under the eye of God. Read as one who has nothing but time.

Before you read, you may wish to pray:

> All-Seeing One,
> above me, around me, within me.
> Be my seeing as I read these sacred words.
> Look down upon me
> Look out from within me
> Look all around me
> See through my eyes
> Hear through my ears
> Feel through my heart
> Touch me where I need to be touched;
>   and when my heart is touched,
>   give me the grace to lay down this Holy Book
>   and ask significant questions:

Why has my heart been touched?
How am I to be changed through this touch?
All-Seeing One,
I need to change
I need to look a little more like You
May these sacred words change and transform me.
Then I can meet You face to face
    without dying
    because I've finally died enough.
To die is to be healed a little more each death,
    until that final death
    when I'll be healed forever.
It will be a healing that will last.
Your Words are healing
    although they bring about my death.

O Eye of God, look not away.

2. . . . *until your heart is touched (Guigo's meditation phase).*

In the Lectio Divina process, meditation begins when your heart is touched. Prayer, being a response to God, is a natural outgrowth of meditation.

Read until your heart is touched. When your heart is touched, stop reading. After all, if God comes in the first verse, why go on to the second? A touched heart means God has, in some way, come. God has entered that heart. Begin your meditation. Meditation is a process in which you struggle with the Word of God that has entered your heart. If this Word wants to be a guest in your heart, go forth to meet it. Welcome it in and try to understand it. Walk with it. Wrestle with it. Ask it questions. Tell it stories about yourself. Allow it to nourish you. Receive its blessing. To do this you must sink your heart into it as you would sink your teeth into food. You must chew it with your heart.

To give you an example of how all this works in the actual process of Lectio Divina, let's say that I am praying with Psalm 61. I come to verse 3, "To the rock too high for me, lead me!" For some reason my heart is touched. I lay my Bible down and slowly repeat that line, "To the rock too high for me, lead me!" Why has this particular phrase edged its way into my heart? I ponder the reason for its coming. Then I recall, there is so much in my life right now that seems too high for me to reach. I need someone to lift me up. I am reminded of an intense new desire, an immense urge, to reach the heights that God has planned for me. This psalm verse is a cry from my heart, a cry for God to lift me to the heights since the experience of life has shown me I can't get there alone.

I use imagery to help me as I pray. Suddenly I see a huge rock far off in the distance. It is as though the rock is rooted in the earth, yet touching the heavens. As I strain to reach the rock an immense bird with kind and shining eyes swoops down and lifts me on her wings. She carries me to the heights. She sets me on the rock and flies away. It feels as though she is still present, although she has gone. I am filled with peace. I keep repeating, "On the rock too high for me to reach, God placed me." This line, in various forms, becomes my prayer-mantra for the day. A mantra is a holy word, a phrase, a sentence that stays in your heart longer and deeper than the rest of your words. It is a crumb, so to speak, out of the whole loaf. You take it with reverence and feed on it. You let it become a song in you throughout the day.

Long after my meditation, when I am mingling with people again, having meetings, typing in my office, driving to a parish workshop, struggling with retreat talks, I remember that prayer. It continues to save me. It continues its breath in me. Each time discouragement sets in, I whisper my prayer-mantra, "On the rock too high for me to reach, set me, lift me up, my God."

That is how I pray with the mantras that come to me from my morning Lectio. Those holy words are my companions during the day, the crumbs I feed on at every hour. They help me

to be more present to those I serve. Over and over I whisper
the holy line until it becomes a part of me. It becomes a Word
made flesh.

Often after moments of frustration and sin when I have not
been present to others, I reflect back on my prayer-mantra for
the day and I realize that if I had fed on it more consistently
throughout the day my lack of presence would not have happened.

You may ask if there is ever a day when my heart is not
touched. Yes, there are many. On some days each psalm or
gospel passage is like the parched earth. There is nothing moist
or life-giving to be found in any words I read. I see this barrenness as a message from God also. On days when nothing
speaks to me, I know that I need to be very quiet. "Be still and
know that I am God." (Ps. 46:10. RSV) God also speaks in silence and darkness. So when nothing comes, when darkness
prevails, then too, I lay my Bible down. My word is silent darkness. I carry the dryness, the emptiness, the silent darkness
with me through the day. It is only in darkness that one can
see the stars. I have seen too many stars to let the darkness
overwhelm me. Even though You are silent, still I will trust You.

3. . . . *until your heart is touched (Guigo's prayer phase).*

In his letter on the contemplative life, Guigo II speaks of
prayer as that phase in the Lectio Divina process in which we
beg of God the fruit of the treasure we've found. Although I
find that description of prayer attractive, I also find it limiting.
Prayer is so much more than begging for a favor. Prayer is a
response to God and to life. It comes from a heart that has been
touched.

How does a touched heart pray? After struggling with the
word that touched it, my heart responds in many different
ways. Sometimes in pure gratitude it simply stands in awe, re-
joicing. And that is prayer! Sometimes it weeps. Sometimes it
sings. There are times it tenderly talks to God. At other times

my heart screams out in anger. Sometimes it looks upon the world with love, or rushes out to do good deeds. Sometimes it kneels with outstretched arms. It turns; it bends and bows. It takes a slow and careful walk. It begs for daily bread. It takes long and grateful looks at everything and everyone. Sometimes it simply yearns for God, or yearns to know itself. All this is prayer!

I strain toward God; God strains toward me. I ache for God; God aches for me. Prayer is mutual yearning, mutual straining, mutual aching. Prayer is the link between meditation and contemplation. Meditation, too, is a form of prayer. All real presence is prayer. In the Lectio Divina process, however, something happens between wrestling with God and disappearing into God that, for me, is prayer at its best. Something happens between chewing and digesting the Word. What happens is tasting and responding. Prayer is tasting life. Prayer is responding to life. Prayer is a very important link between meditation and contemplation. It is a space in between. In all of life, the spaces in between the "bits of life" are of utmost importance.

4. . . . then give yourself up to love (Guigo's contemplation phase).

Giving yourself up to love is melting into God. It is falling into the hands of the living God with complete abandon. This is the deep, interior prayer for which we have been striving. Here we must let go of our dependency on thoughts, words, and images. We go into the beautiful darkness. We stop struggling. We let the angels carry us. Surrender is the only word we know. We let go even of our yearning for God. Nothing is left except being in God. What could I say that would matter when I am in the heart of God? Beautiful darkness! Contemplation! All words are digested. Contemplation is like going to heaven for a while.

When I come back from contemplation I feel very much at peace. I feel as though I have been dead and returned to life, and the life I've come back to isn't quite as full as the death I was in. On some days I have to say, "I didn't quite make it to heaven. I couldn't give up enough of myself to get there."

5. Journaling.

To the Lectio Divina process I add a fifth part, journaling. Getting your heart on paper can be healing. I always write down the prayer-mantra that comes out of my daily reading. That mantra is the one I will carry with me throughout the day. I will breathe it in and out to the four corners of the earth. It will become a friend. Sometimes I begin journaling later in the day after we have become quite known to each other. Sometimes I journal in the morning when I know my mantra less well. Journaling is always a grace for me. In the second part of this book I will share some of my Lectio journal with you.

I journal because it is a way of celebrating my prayer. I journal because it is one way of being present to the life that unfolds on my path each day. I journal because I am filled with thoughts that I must do something with, lest I explode with beauty or pain or yearning. I journal because people come to me seeking ways to be holy, and since I have nothing of my own to give them, writing down what God gives me in prayer can be helpful. I journal because it is a way of saving the graced moments that God gives to me to use in future letters that may be consoling to people in moments of discouragement, pain, or joy.

As Divine Reading becomes a way of life for us, it is easy to see that it is more of a process than a technique. For example, it is not necessary in this process to start with reading. I do not look at reading as the beginning, but rather as part of the process. Being a frequent guest at the table of Scripture, I have enough of the Word of God stored in my heart that I can, at any moment, bring forth food for my prayer. I can begin with meditation or some other aspect of prayer. I can begin by adoring. The secret of Divine Reading is to live my life around the Word of God to such an extent that I am constantly aware of God praying in me. The Word of God becomes at home in me. I am like a portable sanctuary filled with the real presence of God. Being a temple of God, how can I but see God everywhere I look? Within your temple, Lord, I sing about your glory. I am that temple, but you are the glory.

To encourage you to make this prayer process your own, I will review for you now the Lectio Divina process that I use for my prayer. Be as original and creative in your own process as you wish. Let God lead you in this prayer.

1. I begin with reading, if necessary or desired. Ordinarily, I select a specific book of Scripture, a Gospel, or a letter. I often use the Psalms. I read a little each day. Since my goal is not to get finished, it often takes several months to complete the specific work I am praying with. There are times when the readings from the daily liturgy speak so strongly to me that I choose to use those for my Lectio. I have no set plan that is so rigid it cannot be put aside for a while should God decide to come to me through some other channel, like nature or people. We ought not to lock God anywhere, not even in Scripture.

When I am reading, I read until my heart is touched. Sometimes I slowly read an entire chapter. Then I meditate on the words that spoke to me most forcefully. I usually read for a very short time. My heart, when not distracted, is touched quickly and deeply. Sometimes I stop at the moment I feel a stirring within me, a being drawn to the Word. At other times I finish reading the passage and then return to the line that called me to dwell. There are times when I do not read at all. I simply gather some fragments that are left over in my heart from another moment and use them for my daily prayer. One of the "crumbs" that seems to linger in my heart is a line from Psalm 46: "Be still and know that I am God." This prayer and many others are stored in my memory. They are of great assistance to me when I am too weary to read.

2. Once I have chosen my Scripture verse, the line that attracted my heart, it becomes my mantra for the day. I grapple with its meaning for me. I listen to it. I ask God and myself questions about it. I use images. This form of meditation does not require that I surrender images and thoughts. It encourages and welcomes them.

3. Prayer flows naturally out of my meditation. Prayer is actually a part of meditation. Prayer slows me down and nudges me toward letting go of images and thoughts. It directs me toward my Center. It is a movement from active involvement with God to quiet resting in God. It is a gentle slowing down of my inner motor.

4. Contemplation is often spoken of as the highest form of prayer. It is the prayer of heaven. It is the beautiful darkness of trusting God to pray within me. It is interior prayer. Nothing external is left except the shell of my body.

   You may wonder how you can reach that eternal sacred place within where you are simply held by God. It is precisely because you are held by God that you need no thoughts or images of your own. Trust in God's embrace. As you begin your journey into this beautiful darkness, keep saying your prayer-mantra slowly, letting go of a few more words each time. If your mantra is "Be still and know that I am God," you may eventually end up with just the word *still*, or *know*, or *God*. One word is enough to carry you into your sacred Center. Gradually omit even that word. Be aware only of your breathing Your breath is one of the most beautiful prayers that you own. You carry it with you everywhere you go. In order to enter the beautiful darkness, however, you must let go even of the awareness of your breath.

5. Journaling can be done whenever you have the time or feel the call. In the journal selections of this book I share

with you the Scripture verse from my daily reading that touched my heart. In sharing with you my reflection on that verse, I am partially showing you what went on inside of me during my meditation. Not all of my prayer can be shared with you, because sometimes it is a wordless response: tears, silent gratitude, a profound bow, arms outstretched, kneeling with my beggar's bowl, waiting.

My contemplation I cannot show you, nor should I. If my contemplation, my deep being in God, is healthy, it will show up in the way I live my daily life. You will see the results of that contemplation in my life lived out.

This entire Divine Reading process is the most integrated way of praying that I know. That is why at the beginning of this chapter I told you that I was showing you a way to pray that, for me, is pure gold. I see it as pure gold because I see it as a blend of two very rich traditions of spirituality, the Eastern and the Western. I have long felt drawn to the East. What attracts me is the silent, beautiful darkness that seems to get more emphasis in the East than in the West. Looking at the West with a sharper eye, however, I see also that silent, beautiful darkness tucked away in the folds of its history like a treasure hidden in a field. It is waiting to be uncovered. My monastic tradition has somewhat dug it out of the earth for me; yet many around me seem to be starving for the silent beautiful darkness, the treasure of the interior life. In the West it got hidden away in monasteries and convents, and alas, even there it seems to suffer neglect.

In this process of Divine Reading I have discovered the lost treasure of the inner life. It is also the treasure of my lost childhood. There is something naturally Eastern and Western in all of us. The West, at times, seems unaware of a second treasure tucked away within its pages. That is the incarnational aspect and richness of its prayer. Much as I love the silent darkness of the East, I could never give up the earthy, incarnational, creation-centered Western style of prayer. It is a joy to my heart. The first part of the Divine Reading process that I described is a way of prayer in which one is quite involved in the prayer. It is a holy festival of dance and tears, words and images. It is a drama for the soul to delight in and feed upon; but as is only fitting, this holy festival quiets down and melts into silent beautiful darkness. The darkness, the beauty, and the silence are all part of the holy festival. It is *one* prayer spoken to *one* God. It is struggle and rest embracing.

In spirituality today, we often speak of two methods of approaching God known as apophatic and kataphatic. *Apophatic* means away from images. *Kataphatic* means toward images. The Divine Reading process includes both styles. Both styles are used to lead me to the Center. My being with God in quiet darkness is so much richer because I have also been with God in the festival of words and images. My darkness and silence is deeper because I have been involved in the holy activity of bowing and dancing and begging, of gazing and singing and touching.

My experience of Divine Reading began as a child long before I came to know the Scriptures as the Word of God. The Word of God does not wait for scholars to give out information. The Word moves out ahead of the scholars, the adults, seeking open hearts, intent upon transforming souls into the likeness of God.

The spirituality of my childhood is the one I would most like to have restored. It was pure and fresh and honest. I read God everywhere! It was Divine Reading at its best. The forest was my place of solitude. The trees, like gods and goddesses, bent down to hear my prayers. I trusted them with all the secrets of my heart, and I was never disappointed. In their presence I felt safe. Looking back at the poverty and the wealth of my childhood, my memory becomes a ray of hope and pain. I have become too complicated in my prayer. Yet under the eye of God all shall be restored.

IS THERE A LOST CHILD IN YOU?

What pains me most
these days
is my inability
to reach back into my years
and touch the child I was.

And yet,
loving
living
stirring
deep within my soul
that child
lives on.

There are days
when
my adult ways
turn tasteless in my mouth
and the child of long ago
starts
pressing on my soul.

On days like that
I long to touch that child again
and let her take me by the hand
and lead me down
a path that has a heart
and show me all the things
that
I've stopped seeing
because I've grown
too tall.

6. A Handful of Flour, a Little Oil

The stream of our lives has a way of drying up at times, and ravens or angels are not always around to bring us food. The widow of Zarephath (1 Kings, Chapter 17) found herself in this dried-up state. She was gathering sticks to prepare a last meal for herself and her son before they died. It was then that the prophet appeared on the scene, asking for a drink of water. Her poverty did not prevent her from setting off to get the water; but when Elijah asked also for a scrap of bread, she was brought face to face with the reality of her emptiness. It is one thing to be empty, but when you are asked to feed someone out of your emptiness it can be terrifying. Then comes that lovely confession of her utter poverty, "I have only a handful of flour and a little oil . . ." How can you feed someone with so little? The physical poverty and emptiness in this very human, down-to-earth story parallels the spiritual and emotional emptiness that we so often experience at the table of daily life. My hope for you is that you never give up on your handful of flour and your little oil. When you believe in it, the little that you have has tremendous potential to increase. Your jar of meal will not run out. Your little oil shall last forever.

There are days when I stand on this earth with a handful of flour and a little oil knowing full well that with the little I possess I'll never be able to bake a whole loaf of bread. It is then I remember that a little is enough if I bring to it my real presence. When you believe in your little, miracles happen. When you remember the crumbs, wonders abound.

Having eaten my last crumb
I hear a voice in the wilderness of my heart

Bring me a little water
the voice pleads.
I am off for the water
when again I am interrupted
Bring me a scrap of bread
the voice calls.
I freeze inside, barely able to believe
the demands of God.
It is kindness to give someone a drink, yes
But to give out of an empty house is agony.

Someone is asking for a crust of bread
And I have only
a few tears
a handful of flour
a little oil.
The sticks in my hand
are to build a fire,
to bake a few crumbs for myself
before I die.

But the call waits in my soul
like a volcano.
I bake the bread in silence
with my tears
with my handful of flour
with my little oil.
The salt from my tears is the seasoning.

The hungry one eats and is nourished.

Suddenly I am hungry no longer
My vessel of flour is undiminishing
My jar of oil never runs dry.

When you have gathered up the crumbs
of all you have and are
And baked your bread

in the only place left:
the oven of your heart,
Then you will know what it means
to be bread for the world.

There is a wealth in poverty
that ought not to be wasted.
There is a nourishment in crumbs
that ought to be tasted.

In this chapter I share with you the handful of flour and the little oil that have gotten me through many days of famine. My famine ended as I prayed these Scripture passages. I offer you some of the crumbs I have fed on and journaled with.

This is the Scripture portion of my Lectio journal. My journal is my best friend. It is the place where I feel safe to come with my grief and my anger, my joy and delight, my questions, my confusion and frustration, my anxieties, my amazement and awe, my love and ecstacy.

Each mantra that I pray with is only a handful of flour and a little oil; yet I have found it sufficient to change my famine into a feast on many a day. My life has been blessed because I've believed in these crumbs.

> Be a sheltering rock for me
> always accessible . . .
> On you I have relied from birth.
> (Ps. 71:3–6 NJ)

Be a sheltering rock for me! I've never thought of a rock as being very sheltering, but this morning as I sat in prayer I pondered deeply the rocks in my life. One rock in particular stood out from my childhood days. It didn't exactly shelter me from the sun, but it sheltered me from many of the fears in my life. It was like a table where I could sit in moments of sadness. It housed a little spring at its base. That spring became for me water from the rock, though I knew little about Moses in those days. That was, for me, a sheltering rock, always accessible.

Then I thought of another rock in my life. It is a mountain of rock where I can climb to the heights. Leaning against this rock I can be sheltered even from the sun. I can lean on it, climb on it, sit on it. It is a sheltering rock, always there for me. It has become my rock of leisure. It reminds me to *be*.

I remember also my newly discovered rock community in the desert, affectionately called "the place of the Ancient Ones." It is a sacred place made holy with carvings left by the Southwest Indians many years ago. It became a kind of sacred temple for me during my sojourn in the desert.

As I recall these rocks in my life, I think also of the people who have sheltered me. I remember the ones who have shared their homes with me. I remember those who have allowed me to lean on them when my well ran dry.

As I prayed with these rocks this morning, I was brought to a new awareness of how true it is that you, my God, are a sheltering rock in my life, always accessible. You are a rock to lean on, to climb to the heights on, to rest in the shade of. On you I have relied from birth.

The more I rejoice in and understand these rocks in my life, the more I am able to be a rock for others.

Oh God, be a sheltering Rock for me!

Let your tolerance be evident to everyone: the Lord is very near. There is no need to worry; but if there is anything you need, pray for it.

(Phil. 4:5–6)

Let your tolerance be evident to everyone! I've been on this prayer-mantra for four days now. I keep saying it over and over and God keeps saying, "More, more, more! You can be more tolerant, more patient. With me so near, you can do it!"

I sit musing. Really? It doesn't seem to be working. I am so far from being tolerant. I cannot see people the way you see them, my God. I don't have your eyes.

And what's this you say about worry? There is no need to worry? I hear your voice in the psalms too, "Do not fret; it only leads to evil." (Ps. 37:8 Grail) I believe you. Worry has led to nothing but evil in my life. Worry brings lack of peace, restlessness, turmoil. I know it. I know it. But I can't seem to move on into the peace. I can't seem to give up my anxieties. I hear Paul say it again, "There is no need to worry; if you need something pray for it."

I reflect deeply on this passage. Not to worry! Pray instead! I make a change in the wording much to my spiritual advantage. Rather than pray *for* the things I need, I have begun to pray *about* the things I need. When I pray *about* something I widen the possibilities. I look at my intolerance, for example. I look at the reasons for my intolerance, often my own insecurities or my failure to acknowledge my own weaknesses. With God I evaluate the situation. I reflect deeply on it.

When I pray *for* something my prayer tends to be much more narrow. I put expectations on God. I expect something definite to happen and I am disappointed if it doesn't happen. I tend then to look at my prayer as not being answered.

But when I pray *about* something I am putting expectations on myself. I focus on the presence of God in my specific problem and we look at it together, God and I.

Today, dear Lord, I am praying about my intolerance and my anxieties. Come then, my God, let us look at this *together*.

He will transfigure these wretched bodies of ours into copies of his glorious body.

(Phil. 3:21)

At first thought, I revolt at the word *wretched*. I have never really felt wretched, nor do I think God ever looks at me as wretched. However, if I redefine everything, the word *wretched* could mean sinful, weak, finite, limited, grasping, selfish, and so on. I can see that often this poor body of mine is indeed in a sad way and needs to become noble, as is its destiny. This passage from Paul made me sit up straight during my morning Lectio. It got my attention. I have it in me to be a copy of the glorious body of Christ. Most created things are limited to being just what they are, but *me*—ah, I can rise above what I am at this moment. I can transcend.

Today as I walked the fields and roads of our Hesychia House of Prayer, I kept saying, "I can transcend, I can transcend. Christ is going to transfigure my poor, clinging, restless body into a copy of his own glorious body." A quiet silence descended on me as I walked. I walked as one in the heart of a mystery. I felt close to myself in an intimate, healthy kind of way.

Jesus, I know it is true. If I allow you to have full reign in my life, I can transcend. My frail body will take on splendor. I think it's beginning to happen right now.

I can transcend!

Bow down, then, before the power of God. . . . unload all your worries on to him, since he is looking after you.
(1 Pet. 5:7–8)

My greatest worry today is starving. It's embarrassing to admit I am so self-centered, but it happens every time I try to fast. I become so hungry. I want to eat everything in sight. I start thinking about my health and ask myself if I should be fasting—a ridiculous thing to worry about for one as healthy as I. I took a long hard look at this today. Fasting is cleansing when I can be faithful to the challenge. On days when I fast I become so aware of how I ordinarily pamper myself.

Today God took charge of my fasting. As I began to get restless inside and homesick for food, I seemed to hear a quiet voice from within giving me advice. I was told to go outside among the small wild flowers, the pale new green grass, the jonquils and flowering bushes, and to feast on them rather than bemoan my fast.

"Go," God said, "feast on the earth! The blue sky is there for the gazing, the clouds are sprinkled around today like angels waiting to bless you. The breeze is just right. I'm coloring everything up for you just the way you like it. Go have a festival. Feast on everything in sight. Forget your stomach for a while. Think about your heart and soul."

I am sitting here now under the blue, cloudy dome of the sky. I'm feeding on the earth. The sun is gently warming my face. Leftover fall-winter leaves keep blowing around me. New green grass peeps out from a ground that is tired of winter. I feel as though I am at a birth, the delivery of spring.

My stomach has taken second place to all this beauty. My worry of starving to death has diminished. There is food to eat that I so often pass up. Fasting has led me to feasting. I bow down before the Source of All Life. I unload my worries. I feel well taken care of. A wonderful new energy runs through my being. Real presence has turned my fast into a feast. I have bowed down before the power of God.

> **If you, O Lord, should remember our guilt,**
> **Lord, who would survive?**
> *(Ps. 130:3, my paraphrase)*

Today I made a list of all the evils in my life that I would like to eradicate. Often I have not considered such things as these evil. I tend to think evil is something glaring and terribly noticeable, yet so much of the evil in my life is like a cancer that slowly eats me alive. It is good to stand back from it all now and then and ask: How did I get this way? How did I become so suspicious? How did I become so indifferent and apathetic? Where did this unwillingness to look at my faults come from? How did I become so content in the midst of all the trivia of my life? Why am I in this comfortable rut? What evil is lurking in my heart that has brought me to this state? What cancer is eating me alive?

Today, Jesus, I ask you to look at these evils with me. Help me to own them as deadly.

From the evil of fear that traps me in my narrow self-centered existence and prevents me from stepping out in faith and risking new things, deliver me and set me free, Jesus.

From the evil of nearsightedness that confines me to seeing only what is in close and easy reach, deliver me and set me free, Jesus.

From the evil of prejudice that causes me to make judgments about a person or situation before I know all the facts, deliver me and set me free, Jesus.

From the evil of acting omnipotent, trying to do all of God's work alone, and refusing to admit my dependency and poverty, deliver me and set me free, Jesus.

From the evil of busyness and activity, rushing and running the whole day through, never pausing to be still enough that I can experience your contemplative look of love, deliver me and set me free, Jesus.

If you, O Lord, would remember my guilt, how could I survive?

Wash out my hidden faults.

(Ps. 19:12)

The visual image of having my hidden faults washed out is a good one for my prayer today. It does not frighten me at all. I think of the tide coming in and leaving a bit of rubbish on the beach. I feel the same about my faults. If I do have any hidden faults, I'd like to have them washed up, lying at my feet, visible. Why not? I have always looked for truth. I've longed for openness. I want nothing hidden from myself since nothing is hidden from you, my God.

Today, I pray that my hidden faults can be washed up in front of me. Let the tide bring them in. If anything is hidden, it's probably because of denial or blindness. From my secret sins, save me. Why should everyone else know about my sins except me? That's usually the case when I live in denial. I'm ready, God. Let's look at me together. Wash out my hidden faults. Then stand lovingly beside me.

As an eagle incites its nestlings forth by hovering over its brood, so he spread his wings to receive them and bore them up on his pinions. *(Deut. 32:1–12)*

My parent God has done the same for me. He found me in a wilderness. It was the wilderness of my own shallow life. It was my desert of illusions. He enticed me forth. He called me to new heights.

She hovered over me, spreading out her wings to receive me. She asked me to let go of my empty and false gods. With her love for nurturing and her eye for protection, God is both Mother and Father to me. Continually, she carries me to the heights.

When I remember this eagle flight of my life I feel so loved and so in love. I am cherished. I feel gratefully safe. I can only call out, "Take me to the heights and I'll learn to fly." You, my God, spread forth wings to bear me up.

You have seen . . . how I carried you on eagles' wings and brought you to myself.

(Exod. 19:4)

I remember my first call to greatness. I couldn't put it all together at the time, for I was quite young. Later in my adult life, when I meditate on this and reflect backward I definitely see it as a call to greatness. It was the day I first longed for wings.

"Mom," I said, "I wish I had wings like the birds. I wish I could fly." "God made you the way he wanted you," my mother suggested. "If God had wanted you to have wings he would have given you wings."

It was a sad answer, I thought, and I went off quietly to my secret rock table to ponder the matter. Perhaps I was feeling limitation for the first time. My feet were glued to the earth. My desire for wings has never completely left me. It is one of my better desires. Secretly, it wants to lift me off the earth. I am not to get root-bound. I have come to believe that second best, next to flying, is wanting to fly. And I suspect that to get off this earth, someday my soul will sprout wings and I will, after all of this waiting, finally be able to fly.

I have seen how you carried me on eagles' wings and brought me to yourself. And so I pray for wings of my own.

Give me a drink.

(John 4:7)

Oh, for the wisdom to ask for the drink that I need, the drink that will save me. It is raining this morning, a quiet, steady flow. And so I am reminded of drinks, free drinks from my Parent God, my Father and my Mother. I let the rain soak into my mind and heart as it soaks into the earth. I feel saturated with the need for a drink. I hear Jesus asking the woman at the well for a drink. What a humble, beautiful request. God asking a woman for a drink! Divinity requesting a drink from humanity! Heaven asking earth for a drink! Sitting here watching the raindrops slide down my window, I hear Jesus say, "Give me a drink." An awesome request!

And I pray, Jesus, take away the fear that prevents me from asking for the drinks I need. Take away the blindness that prevents me from recognizing the drinks I need.

The drink of life! Union with God! Jesus, give me a drink. Give me your life.

You have no bucket and the well is deep: How could you get this living water?

(John 4:11)

I guess you don't need a bucket when the living water is flowing through you. The well is deep and each of us is a well if only we could see and understand. *We are a well*! We were made for the deeps. Christ lives in the depths of us. This *woman* at the well, who is all of us, didn't understand. She was thinking of only one kind of water, the water that quenches our thirst as we come huffing and puffing to the mountaintop.

So what do you say to someone without a bucket who tells you, while sitting beside a well, that he'll give you living water if only you will ask? "You're going to give me living water? You don't have a bucket and this well is deep." Not a bad answer, I'd say! You do need something to get the water out of the well. And this leads me to take a look at my buckets. What are the buckets in my spiritual life? What are the tools that I use to dip down deep into the well of my life to draw out the living water?

One of my favorite buckets is the prayer of Lectio Divina. Divine Reading! It has been my best friend in getting me to the living waters—so much so, that after a while I don't need it anymore. Process that it is, it just unfolds in me. I feel and experience the living water of God's Word whether I open the Scriptures or not. All I need to do is sit by the well. All I need to do is be the well. Let the waters flow through me and be in touch. Be present. However, as beginners, we do need buckets. As humans, we need buckets. Frail mortals that we are, we find it difficult to be in touch with the living water at every moment. Buckets, then, are those tools that I use to get to the flowing source of life.

Some of my favorite buckets in life have been friends. A good listener is a wonderful bucket. To sit at someone's feet and listen to his or her wisdom is one way to reach the living water. Many cherished prayer forms serve as buckets: Centering prayer, the Jesus Prayer, the Rosary, the Eucharist, various forms of meditation. All these and more are buckets along the way. Perhaps the very best of buckets is the practice of real presence. Being present to life is a marvelous way to stay in touch with living water. God's grace is more available than we dare to believe. It's a bit like the little fish who swam up to its mother and asked, "What is the ocean?" "You're in it," said the mother. But the little fish swam away disappointed, saying, "No, this is just water. I want to know what the ocean is."[1]

My meditation today tells me to be careful before proclaiming that someone doesn't have a bucket. They just might *be* the bucket! I'm also taking a look at my buckets. I am giving thanks for everything and everyone that has been a bucket for me, leading me to the deeps. Neophite that I am, I still need buckets.

Whoever drinks this water will get thirsty again; but anyone who drinks the water I shall give will never be thirsty again: the water that I give will turn into a spring welling up eternal life.

(John 4:14)

Today I met a spring. It was as though something was "welling up" inside of her. I felt that I was in a holy presence. And now, tonight, I pray with the *why* of it all. Why? Why did I experience such a special presence? Perhaps it was because she has drunk deeply of that fountain within. Perhaps she has not denied it as I so often do.

All of us have such possibilities for becoming springs of living water. O God, be merciful to my distracted way of living. I want to be a well!

Sir, give me some of this water, so that I may never get thirsty and never have to come here again to draw water.

(John 4:15)

How easy it is to ask for living water for the wrong reason. How easy it is to get the plain, natural water confused with the living water. Still, I begin with the natural. It, too, is charged with the sacred. It leads me to a deeper search, for as my human thirst is quenched with well water I become aware that no matter how often I drink from this natural stream, there is still an unquenched thirst in me.

Jesus knew about this unquenched thirst as he spoke with the woman. He knows about this deeper thirst as he talks to me each day. To get me to look at this deeper thirst, he sometimes asks startling questions or gives clinching commands. And so, to the woman, he said, "Go call your husband." The statement is different for each person, but it is a statement that coaxes you to look into your soul. The "Go call your husband" statement is one that makes you squirm a bit. It could just as well be "How's your mother?" or "Where is your heart?" It leads us within, where we are forced to take an honest look at our lives.

**The hour is coming when you will worship neither on this
mountain nor in Jerusalem. . . . True worshipers will worship the
Father in spirit and truth.**

(John 4:22–24)

What a revelation! The hour is coming when you will worship out of who you are. The hour is coming when you will
realize that the spirit and the truth live within you. You are a
portable chapel. Remember the sanctuary within. You carry
God wherever you go. Why quarrel about churches, temples,
or mountains? One particular place isn't necessarily holier than
another.

I recall, however, that throughout the ages, special events
have made places holy and we ritualize that holiness in many
ways. That's why Abraham was always stacking up stones, cre-
ating altars in the places where God visited him. It was a way
of celebrating a special event and a special place that had become sacred because of an encounter with God. It's the encounter that we must remember even more than the place. We
humans sometimes put too much emphasis on the place. Places
are important, but I do pray we will never lose the spirit of that
encounter, for it is that spirit that will heal us.

There are places where I could stack up my stones and pour
on my oil. Holy places! I will never forget them. Neither will I
forget the altar within. I carry my chapel wherever I go. I am
your temple, God, and in baptism this frail temple of mine was
consecrated, dedicated to you, the Most High God of heaven
and earth. How well I understand your words to me today,
Jesus. The hour is coming when I will worship in spirit and
truth.

**The woman put down her water jar and hurried back to tell the
people.**

(John 4:28)

She put down her water jar. This very well may be the heart
of this beautiful story. Her water jar is her own agenda. It's the
reason she came to the well. She came to draw water. She came

for natural water. She left with eternal life. She walked away from that well with living water because she was able to let go of her own agenda. She was able to put down the water jar of her own agenda and go forth with God's agenda. She forgot the water jar. Her own need for her natural thirst to be quenched suddenly wasn't all that important, for she had come to experience the quenching of a much deeper thirst in her encounter with Jesus. She put down her water jar and she went out to tell the good news. She brought other people to the well, and so, to Jesus. She became a bucket, a means of bringing others to the living water.

Jesus, give me the courage to put down my water jar. My agenda is getting heavy in my life. I want to go with your agenda for me. I want to be a well!

We no longer believe because of what you told us; we have heard him ourselves, and we know that he really is the savior of the world.
(John 4:42)

This is the place to which I long to come in my faith journey. It is that place in which I come to know out of my own experience that Jesus is Lord and Savior. The day will come when I must say to my grandparents, my parents, my teachers, "No longer does my faith depend on your story. I have seen and heard for myself. Now I know. This is the savior of the world. I have experienced God. It is my own experience, not just something I heard from the altar. No longer does my faith depend on your story. It's within. I've become a well!"

And when that day comes I'll also give thanks for all those buckets who brought me to this welling moment.

I stretch out my hands,
like thirsty ground I yearn for you.
(Ps. 143:6)

Like thirsty ground I am yearning for you, but you do not come. I feel angry because of this Divine Absence.

It is the story of my life. I neglect you for days. But I expect you to be here like morning sunshine when I remember you again. Yes, there are times when my heart becomes numb with getting used to you, so numb that it feels like a great void. Then I blame you for your absence. All this week I have felt smothered by your disappearance. If the truth be known, it is I who have become too casual about you, God. I let the fire that you are escape my notice. I let the wonder in me die. There is nothing more deadly than getting used to the Beloved.

You were long in coming today, my God. I expected you to be present in glory at the snap of my fingers, at the longing of my heart, even though I've kept you safely in heaven for days. Today when I began to look for you I came to realize that I was no longer in the habit of searching for you in deep places. When my thirsty ground started longing for you I closed my eyes and began to look.

This in itself is an interesting phenomenon. When I want to see clearly I close my eyes. That says something very powerful about another kind of seeing that instinctively I know I have. It says something about my inner eye that I've not used for a while. Today I came to realize that my inner eye has suffered from neglect. It has suffered from underuse. It needs recharging. My life with God has suffered because I've not been present to this inner eye.

O God of tender mercies, I know I've kept you at arm's length. I've kept you safe in heaven. But heaven has leaned down to the earth and I've been touched anew. Like thirsty ground I long for you. Forgive my casualness about your Love. Forgive my shallow life. I am finished with shallowness. I used to pray that I be saved from eternal death, but now I pray to be saved from shallow living. Eternal death? Shallow living? Is there a difference? O God, deliver me from shallow living!

In the course of their journey he came to a village, and a woman named Martha welcomed him into her house. She had a sister called Mary, who sat down at the Lord's feet and listened to him speaking.
(Luke 10:39)

Today I have such a desperate longing to find wise people, to sit at their feet, to listen to their wisdom. It is consoling to know that Jesus told Mary she had chosen the better part when he found her sitting at his feet. Dinner can always wait. If you find someone holy, forget dinner . . . there is a deeper nourishment than can be found at the dinner table. It is this deeper kind of feeding that we are all hungering for.

It has been such a struggle to get the Mary and Martha balanced in my life. Both are so important. They are the *ora et labora* in the rule of Saint Benedict. Bernard of Clairvaux blesses me further by reminding me that Mary and Martha are sisters and they live in the same house. I experience them in my house at every moment. The dilemma is, How do I feed Mary and how do I feed Martha? Perhaps the more important question is, How do I teach them to feed each other?

Jesus, help me to know when to sit at your feet and when to fix dinner.

You, O Lord, are my lamp, my God who lights my darkness.
With you I can break through any barrier,
With my God I can scale any wall.

(Ps. 18:29 Grail)

These words came leaping into my heart during my desert day. At first they seemed a bit much for me to take in. After all, when has my God been so powerfully present in my life that I felt as though I could break through any barrier? I prayed the words again and almost choked on them.

I placed the words in my memory and prayed them again and again. I stood at the window gazing at the winter sky. All the while I kept repeating, "You are my lamp. You light my darkness. With you I can break through any barrier. With you I can leap any wall." Then the tears came. I did not fully understand them but I let them come. I did not fight them. They were wonderfully healing. I remembered that somewhere in the Psalms it says that God has all my tears stored in a flask. I smiled through my tears and prayed, "My God, if you've kept all my tears, heaven is going to be pretty wet."

You are the One who lights my darkness. And when my darkness doesn't get lit, which happens quite often, then my idols have taken over. My lamp is no longer my God. It happens often in my life and I know it. I feel it deep inside. My idols stand there, possessing me, blocking the divine light. I think that's why the tears came. My tears know more than I know. That's why it's so important to listen to them, to pray with them.

I trust in people a lot. I depend too much on human flesh. God tells me that's not where I should place my trust. At this particular moment in my life these words are especially powerful. I am in an unlit moment, and the moment keeps getting longer. And so I did what I so often do in life's hard moments. I turned to a person. I really believed that in sitting at that person's feet I would find my answer in the darkness. I believed that sitting at her feet, my lamp would be relit. But it so happened that my human savior was in the desert herself. Her lamp was unlit, too. I was not prepared for that. I like the saviors I turn to, to have their lamps trimmed and ready. This meeting in darkness turned out to be an unexpected grace, a crumb of great nourishment. Now I know that two people with unlit lamps can give hope to one another as they remember together the One who is their Light.

This evening as my sunset becomes a sunrise for someone else, I repeat once again my day's mantra, "You, O Lord, are my lamp, my God who lights my darkness . . ." In the praying of these few lines I have found sufficient nourishment on this desert day. It is true that I never finished my office today. God came on the twenty-ninth verse. If God comes on the twenty-ninth verse, forget about the thirtieth verse. We miss so much when we try to finish everything, even prayer. Prayer is life. It cannot be finished.

They have taken the Lord out of the tomb, and we don't know where they have put him. *(John 20:2)*

I stood beside the tomb weeping. The tomb was my heart. Peering inside I saw an angel. Ah, at least a bit of the divine— an angel in my heart! The One I love is making certain that even when he's gone there's a guest in my heart. The angel looked at me. "Why are you weeping?" she asked.

Why am I weeping! They have taken away the One I love and I haven't the slightest clue about where they put him.

Then turning, I saw a stranger. "Are you responsible for his absence?" I asked. The stranger spoke my name. I knew the voice, but before I could touch him, he said to me: "Do not cling to me. Do not cling to your past images of me. Do not cling to a mere part of me. Do not cling to the moment when I was closest to you, or when I was most absent. Do not cling to multiplied loaves, calmed seas, water changed into wine, with- ered fig trees, or blind people seeing again. To cling to any one image of me will never be enough for you. Do not cling to what you once knew of me.

"I call you to let go of even good things—of even good im- ages of me—in order to *be me* more completely. And I promise in those moments of near despair when you look for me and can't find me—and there will be many—to leave an angel in your heart to help convince you that I'm alive.

"Now go! Go and live me. But do not cling to me. If you cling to me you will never *be me* in the world. I ask for nothing less than total transformation. It will not be easy. It will not be soon. But *cheer up*; there's an angel in your heart."

Let dawn bring news of your faithful love.

(Ps. 143:8 paraphrase)

The angels came at dawn bringing news of God's faithful love. They woke me early for a change. They unplugged my ears so I could hear the glorious song of the birds. They wiped the sleep out of my eyes so I could see the silhouette of trees celebrating the dawn and the first rays of sun shimmering through the clouds. My nose was then unclogged so the aroma of dawn—from crisp autumn leaves to fresh morning coffee— could delight me. The air at the tips of my fingers reminded me of the gift of touch. My hand clasped around my coffee cup felt warm and welcoming. The taste of the coffee and the freshness of dawn lingered in my mouth as I began my Morning Watch. The touch of my knees on the floor felt right. I knelt with joy. My heart, now fully awakened, sang praises to God's faithful love.

O Beloved One in the heavens and in my heart, always-always, *please*, send angels at dawn, for life is not always so good as it tasted this morning.

7. A Tree Full of Angels

My morning stroll has taken me farther than I had intended. Sauntering up the hill, wading through the autumn leaves, I breathe in the crisp morning air. It is just dawn. Standing still for a moment, I see the first rays of sunlight shimmering through a silver maple tree. It is truly a moment of wonder, resplendent with light. I stand gazing as one in the midst of a vision. Suddenly I am uncertain whether those golden arms swaying in the morning sunlight are tree branches or angel wings. Such shining I find overpowering. My wondering heart is filled with joy.

And then in a twinkling I'm certain. I am standing before a tree full of angels dazzling me with their glorious presence. Bright wings of fire all aglow. Such beauty! Celestial bodies trembling in the trees! Trembling in awe over the beauty of a world that I take for granted. A tree bespangled with glory! Radiant Light! Angel wings, like stars, glistening in every branch. It's gold and silver everywhere I look.

So what do I do? What do I do with this vision that heaven has blessed me with? If I am an adult I keep very quiet about this vision, carefully guarding my reputation. I tell no one. If I am a child, or if I have a child's heart, I cannot contain the vision. I shout it from the rooftops. I say, "Listen, everybody! I saw a tree full of angels shining like stars in the night."

Can you not believe this? Come now, don't be a cynic. Your heart was made for deep things. Your entire being was designed for visions. But if you cannot believe, you are not alone in your unbelief. William Blake's father had some difficulty, too.

It happened to William Blake once when he was rambling over the hills of Dulwich. Being yet a mere child he was not inhibited about his vision and ran quickly to tell his parents the joyful tidings. "I saw a tree filled with angels." His father was about to punish him for telling lies. But his mother, whose heart was less divided and so more able to see to the depths of things, saved him. She rescued him from his father's blindness.

It is so like adults not to be able to tell the difference between a vision and a mirage.

Artists are those who have visions. There is something of the artist in each of us. Artists have hungry eyes and hungry hearts, and on some days when they are purifying their eyes and hearts for deeper seeing, they choose to have hungry stomachs as well. Fasting empties them so that they can see the truth more clearly.

The poets and the saints, artists of all kinds, are ripe for visions because they are always hungry. They are hungry for truth. Their entire beings are filled with hunger, hunger to know, to understand, to create. They are hungry to see to the depths of things. They are not satisfied with our ordinary dim way of seeing.

A wonderful example of our dim way of seeing is given in Thornton Wilder's play *Our Town*.[1] Emily, who has died, wants to come back to the land of the living and relive one day of her life. The stage manager knows the heartache she will experience and is not enthusiastic about her request, but Emily is determined. She chooses her twelfth birthday to return. It is indeed a heartache as she sees how myopic human beings really are, how they simply do not have time to look at one another. At one point she pleads with her mother to look at her for just one moment with undistracted eyes.

Watching so much loveliness going on in the midst of such blindness proves to be too much for her. In desperation she asks to return to her grave. Tearfully, she asks if any human beings ever fully realize life while they live it. The stage manager gives a sad "No," and then as if remembering the redeemers of the human race, he suggests that the poets and saints came closest to tasting the fullness of life.

In the section of my journal that I share with you in this chapter, I am praying with the saints and poets. I am feeding on their vision, their questions, and their dreams.

I have never been one to limit God to the Scriptures, though the Scriptures have nourished me well. My God is not imprisoned anywhere, not in the Bible nor the tabernacle. Real Presence is everywhere, and those with the hearts of children revel in it. So much that I do not blush to call divine is revealed to me each day. The Word and the Bread! That's all there is. They continue becoming flesh. A crumb at a time!

> Tyger! Tyger! burning bright
> In the forest of the night,
> What immortal hand or eye
> Could frame thy fearful symmetry?
>
> In what distant deeps or skies
> Burnt the fire of thine eyes?
> On what wings dare he aspire?
> What the hand dare seize the fire?
> William Blake[2]

Where does the Creator get the fire that burns in my eyes? This brand new question was born this morning during my prayer.

I used to read this poem as a simple little poem about a tiger. Now as I pray it, rather than just read it, I see that it is a magnificent hymn of praise and triumph. The Creator and the tiger sing this hymn together.

Praying this poem has been like being in the audience at the moment of creation. The Creator is wildly intent on bringing forth this fierce and wonderful creature. I feel the respect that the Creator has for the tiger.

As I read between the lines, some of the fierce wonder of the mysterious unnamed Creator becomes a part of the tiger. I can almost see Blake holding this poem in his heart, his eyes moving back and forth from the Creator to the creature, loving them both, marveling over both.

In my meditation I see the awesome, passionate Creator lifting the tiger out of the fire. Both tiger and Creator are trembling with awe. I know that whatever comes through fire is perfected. Yet this moment of being lifted out of the fire is even deeper.

The tiger becomes the fire, the fire of life. What hand could dare seize this fire? Both creature and Creator are burning with life.

And then we come to a lovely question in the poem. When the great Artist twisted the sinews of the tiger's heart, heard the heart begin to beat, grasped this terrifying wonder in his hands, did he smile to see his work?

> Did he smile his work to see?
> Did he who made the lamb make thee?

No answer is expected. Reverent silence is more appropriate.

Somehow this creation story is my own story, and I am still pondering my initial question: Where does the Creator get the fire that burns in my eyes? This question needs no answer either, though I suspect the fire is from heaven. It is enough to pray one's questions and rest quietly in the possibilities. My life is too small for all the answers, and my life, like Blake's, has been plagued with the need for too much certainty.

It is enough to suspect that the fire burning in my eyes and in my soul is a holy fire. It is enough to live in such a way that those who observe me, suspect that I've been through the fire. It is enough to wonder how the divine Artist felt when the first beat of my heart was heard in heaven. It is enough to believe that Blake's unnamed Creator, whom I call God, reached through the flames trembling with awe and turned me, like the tiger, loose in the world. It is enough for me to stand on the earth trembling with awe until I am lifted to the heavens. The lifting begins the moment my feet touch the earth. Birth is a process. Heaven is, too.

> A Robin Red Breast in a Cage
> Puts all Heaven in a rage . . .
> A Skylark wounded in the wing
> A Cherubim does cease to sing.
> William Blake[3]

Is it so strange that heaven should rage and angels stop singing when life is imprisoned or wounded? All life is precious. Heaven cherishes life. The dream of heaven-folk is that earth-folk will learn to hold life dear. I learned to cherish life in the second grade and I haven't forgotten. It was the turtles who taught me.

Today I carried all the images of life that I could hold in my mind's eye: trees and flowers, bees, mourning doves and turtles, geese and eagles, deer and rabbits, lions and tigers and bears, men and women, children and angels, and of course, God, the Life of all life. Such beautiful memories of life filled my soul. Moments from the past visited the empty places in my heart and renewed my reverence for life.

One special memory from childhood days lingers. It is the memory of all the turtles I saved from untimely death. Crossing the roads at their contemplative pace proved to be pure danger as the cars would go racing by. It seemed a noble deed to place them safely across the road. I would carefully check to see which way the turtle was traveling, because I did not want to undo the fruits of my loving kindness by putting it back from where it had come. Whether the turtles appreciated my great care on their behalf I do not know, but it did make me feel a little like God. A savior and a protector! Are we not made in the image of God? It seems right to act the part.

This urge to save turtles has stayed with me in adult years, though I do it less frequently. Sometimes the illusion that we are busy and do not have time for such trifles sets in with adulthood. It is a pity, and I am less human and less holy for all my racing around, yet I race on.

There are moments, though, when I am blessed to remember heaven's rage and the angels' lost song. I forget, for a moment, about my great importance and busyness. I pull to the side of the road and carry God's turtle to safety. If we should think that God doesn't care about the life of that one turtle, then we really don't know God at all.

If God has such a heart for turtles and sparrows, robins and skylarks, I can faintly imagine the depth of heaven's heartbeat for those of us who have been created in the divine image.

By dint of suffering this woman, a living and strong, courageous Christian has learned that there is only one way of making contact with God and that this way . . . is poverty.

Leon Bloy[4]

My heart holds no resistance to this difficult but lovely passage. These are exactly the words sent to me for my morning prayer on this day of fasting. The only way to make contact with God is through poverty. If I am too full of myself, I will never find God.

Johannes Metz, in his little book *Poverty of Spirit*, echoes the words of the woman who was poor when he suggests that we have only two choices in life: to accept our innate poverty or to be a slave to anxiety.[5]

I have been a slave to anxiety far too long. Anxiety robs me of my peace. It comes from forgetting that I am not in control. The moments when I have been most deeply in touch with God are those moments when I have been able to embrace my utter poverty. When I accept my poverty, my total dependence on God, I become vulnerable and God can more easily reach me because I'm not so busy resisting being reached. When I am not resisting my poverty, I can more easily experience God in other people also, for I am more willing to allow them to minister to me. I am able to sit at their feet. Until we learn to sit at one another's feet, we will starve at our lavish banquet tables.

In this early morning stillness, I am embracing my poverty as gift. I am so aware of how I hide from my innate poverty. But this morning my emptiness is helping me feel mellow rather than afraid. I feel like a vessel whose emptiness is part of its beauty. I see the many ways I've tried to hide from my poverty.

How often I've used my possessions to hide from my poverty! I try to fill up the gnawing ache in my life with material things, but the emptiness remains. Sometimes I use words to hide from my poverty. I chatter on with so much trivia. I get lost in the illusion of the importance of my words, words that begin to oppress rather than heal. Then there are the times when I use my busyness to hide from my poverty. If I am in the midst of a flutter of activity I do not have to feel my poverty. I numb myself to God's grace with my ceaseless activity.

This morning my busyness, my words, and my possessions have little value. I am content to be an empty vessel, and I know that the very best way to reach God is through my littleness. This morning I am content to be poor. May this morning last!

It is not what you are nor what you have been that God sees with his all-merciful eyes, but what you desire to be.
The Cloud of Unknowing [6]

Today was a sad day. It wasn't a harsh, overwhelming sadness. It was more like a soft, gentle sadness that settled in my soul and refused to allow me to be apathetic. It was a sorrowing presence hovering around me, urging me to deeper living.

Noontime came and I felt drawn to retire quietly to my room for a few moments of prayer. I began to pray the office of Noonday Praise. When I came to the Psalm line "I am a pilgrim on earth . . ., (Ps.119:19 Grail)" tears began welling up in my eyes. I felt overcome with grief. The grief centered around my monastic vocation. It seemed such a pity to have been in monastic life for almost twenty-five years and still be so very far from holiness. It seemed a scandal that my heart was still so divided and my life so cluttered with trivia. My monastic profession, with its call to become a brand new person in Christ and its invitation to let the old shell of myself crumble away, stood before me with pleading eyes.

Then as quickly as the intense grief had come, it was suddenly gone. A quiet grief remained. It was a healing grief. I had never felt anything akin to it. I saw before me so much potential for my life, so much possibility.

I understand now that it can be a good prayer to weep over the person you've refused to become. Jesus did it for us when he wept over Jerusalem, but there's nothing like feeling the salt on your own face. Yet while you are weeping, it is imperative that you remember the seed of eternal life that is yours, even if you have not yet become all you can be.

Tonight as I reflect on this experience, I have no doubt that my sorrowing heart is a gift from God. As I pray with *The Cloud of Unknowing*, these words are given to me: "It is not what you are nor what you have been that God sees with his all-merciful eyes, but what you desire to be."

My yearning for God has been so deep lately. It's been an ache that I cannot reach. Today the God I couldn't reach, reached me—reached into my inner soul and showed me my speck of eternal life.

Yearning for God is not safe if you want to stay as you are. If you yearn for God, a sacred presence will begin to fill you. It will hover over you, nudging you to a new and eternal life. It will mean, of course, a radical change from your old lifestyle, for God will come and upset your entire life with a haunting presence, a presence that is both terrible and beautiful. It will be a terrible beauty.

With all-merciful eyes, God sees what I desire to be. And though I ache because of the person I've refused to be, I also rejoice because of the person I long to be. I know that my yearning has reached heaven.

> God, devil and the world all wish to enter me
> Of what great lineage my noble heart must be.
> *Angelus Silesius*[7]

I took my noble heart for a walk this morning and pondered the truth of these words. Everyone seems to be warring for my soul and on some days I feel the struggle more intensely than on others.

Yes, of what great lineage my noble heart must be! It is good to think about one's nobility on occasion. Today at Morning Praise just as the sun was rising we sang these words: "Your noblest task is to adore . . ." Those beautiful words gave flesh to my morning walk. I walked as one ready to bow and to adore. It surely helps to cheer up the morning when one is positive about life. To embrace my nobility instead of always wallowing in my corruption feels so right to me. I think that must be part of the reason God came to us in Jesus, to embrace our frail human flesh as good and perhaps to give us our inheritance early.

Ah! My noble lineage! Have I come from God? Perhaps I have, for there is a part of me that seems to remember stars I cannot reach. And I've never felt very much at home here on earth. With C. S. Lewis I cry out, "If I find in myself a desire which no experience in this world can satisfy, the most probable explanation is that I was made for another world."[8]

I must guard this holy temple well. If the spirit of God, the spirit of evil, and the spirit of the world are all clamoring for space in the temple that I am, I must walk with a watchful eye, remembering my noble lineage. My inheritance, like a treasure hidden in a field, lies near unclaimed. Unclaimed inheritance and forgotten nobility can only lead to a life impoverished.

O God, save me from impoverishment. It seems so foolish to starve in a land of plenty.

I feel as if I were the guardian of a precious slice of life with all the responsibility that entails. There are moments when I feel like giving up or giving in but I soon rally again and do my duty as I see it: to keep the spark of life inside me ablaze.

Etty Hillesum[9]

To keep the spark of life inside me ablaze! What a precious responsibility! I had never thought of it quite like that before, as part of my vocation. But why not? If the spark of life in me is ablaze, that means I am full of enthusiasm, and to be full of enthusiasm means to be possessed with God.

Etty's voice comes to us out of the tragedy of the Holocaust. The diary of this remarkable Jewish woman who died at Auschwitz in November 1943, at the age of twenty-nine, convinces me of an amazing inner strength we all possess. Have we ever met our inner strength? Do we know the secret of connecting with it? What do we do with the slice of life that has been entrusted to our care?

Yes, Etty, I, too, am the guardian of a precious slice of life. If I were, like you, guarding this precious life in the face of hostility, a few days away from being sent to a concentration camp, I really don't know if I could be so amazingly positive. Your spirit enriches me. I want that same life-embracing spirit that you carried within your being. It is easy to embrace life when the sun is shining, but when the gloom is on, that's another story.

The dangers from which I must guard my slice of life are more subtle than those you faced during your days in the camp, but just as harmful.

There is the danger of apathy and complacency, living my life overly satisfied with things as they are. I have an amazing ability, at times, to settle for shallow living.

There is the danger of blindness, not seeing with my inner eye. How harmful it is for me to see only that which does not threaten me. Yet how often I refuse to look at the very things that would call me out of my frigid safety.

There is the danger of negativism, becoming overly critical of every little fault. It is like being a living no to life's possibilities. All of these dangers eat away at me a little more each day, making the flame that I am a little dimmer.

Etty, my sister, and Jesus, my brother, in some strange way you both died on a cross. You died believing in life, believing in the ones who killed you. Help me to keep the spark of life in me ablaze.

It still all comes down to the same thing. Life is beautiful. And I believe in God. And I want to be there right in the thick of what people call "horror" and still be able to say: Life is beautiful. . . . I don't think I have nerves of steel, far from it, but I can certainly stand up to things. I am not afraid to look suffering straight in the eyes.

Etty Hillesum[10]

I always say that winter is my fourth favorite season. It is not first, to be sure, yet there is something in it that I favor. I need the scourging that it brings. I need its toughness and endurance. I need its hope. I love the way winter stands there saying, "I dare you not to notice my beauty." What can I say to a winter tree when I am able to see the shape of its soul because it has finally let go of its protective leaves? What do you say to an empty tree? Standing before an empty tree is like seeing it for the first time. Oh, the things that can be seen when one is empty.

Are our lives so very different when we're empty? When we've turned loose our protective coverings, is our beauty any less? In the seasons of life, suffering is my fourth favorite season. I could not place it first, yet like winter, there is something in it that has my favor. It is not easy to be praying about suffering while the sun is rising, but I try not to turn away from what God asks me to gaze upon. My sunrise is someone else's sunset. My cry of joy stands beside someone else's cry of sorrow. They are two seasons of the same life.

Etty, my sister, there was something about you that was glorious even before you died. That same bit of glory is in each of us, yet we are so reluctant to claim it as our inheritance.

You were not afraid to stand in the middle of what people call "horror" and still proclaim that life is beautiful. I tremble at your proclamation. My eyes fill with tears. This is feminine energy at its best. This is the spiritual energy that has the power to heal the world. You were not afraid to look suffering straight in the eye, showing another face of feminine energy—a quiet, knowing strength.

There is something about suffering that is ennobling. I've seen it recreate people. I've seen the mystery of suffering unfold people in a way that is sacramental, giving them the face of Christ. I have watched people suffer and I've wondered. I've wondered what it is that gifts people with the courage to suffer so well. What is it that makes some people able to embrace suffering in such a way that they are lifted up rather than crushed? What is this secret and mysterious energy, this seed planted in the heart of the human race?

And why is it that some of us learn how to embrace suffering in a way that makes us beautiful? And why is it that some of us allow it to embitter us? We were all formed out of the same kind of clay. What makes us so different?

O God, help me, like Etty, to be able to stand in the thick of suffering still remembering that life is beautiful. Help me to embrace all of life so that I am ennobled, lifted up and changed into Christ. Give me the courage to look all of life straight in the eye. Give me the courage of the saints.

I feel called to something "more"—something bigger than me— bigger than my own recovery. It's not that I don't want healing—It's just that that is not all there is.

Marilyn Schwab[11]

It is hard to stand at the bedside of one who is dying and say, "There is something bigger than recovery," and yet when the one who is dying says it, it is awesome.

Would that at the moment of my death I could have the vision to pray Marilyn's prayer, "I feel called to something more, something bigger than me, even bigger than healing."

Could it be that if we really understood death we would see it as the deepest healing of all? Is death the great healing? Is our life on earth partially a wound that death finally heals?

Saint Benedict tells us to keep death daily before our eyes. Walk with death as a friend. I am trying to remember the great healing daily. I am trying to look at death not as a dark and dreadful foe but as an usher into a new life.

Solitude means being lonely not in a way that pleases you but in a way that frightens and empties you to the extent that it means being exiled even from yourself.

Thomas Merton[12]

Few of us have the courage for real solitude. Few of us have the courage to lay down our words and sit silently with empty hands, empty minds, empty hearts. Few of us have the courage to embrace the poverty of being utterly alone. Alone! All one! Being alone means being all one. All one with God! For me that is a beautiful and terrifying thought. It means disappearing into God. It means that I am lost in God. I am exiled from myself and can be found only in God. To be exiled from the self that I know into the God I do not know, but who knows me, is frightening. It is, in fact, a dying to myself. It is my greatest hope for eternal life and yet I fear it. To be exiled from myself is the greatest of detachments.

Yearning for solitude, I have come to realize that I am yearning to be a person rather than an individualist. If I am a person, I am hidden with Christ in God. If I am an individualist, I am hidden only in my own false self. There is a significant difference between a person and an individualist. No one says this better than Thomas Merton: "True solitude is the home of the person. False solitude is the refuge of the individualist."[13]

I learn who I am most of all by examining my motives. I often ask myself now as I sit alone in my cell, "Is this a home or a refuge? Am I just alone, or am I all one with God?"

Alone
All-one
Alone with God
All-one with God
Being alone with God
Being all-one with God
All-one
Alone.

It is a terrible grace.
An awesome gift,
but terrifying all the same.
There is no way to get there
except to lose yourself,
to lose what you know of yourself.

And then, the battle is over.
There will be nothing left but God.

Being alone, all-one, with God
is a terrible and beautiful grace.
Terrible, because
the only way there
is to lose yourself.

Beautiful, because
when you lose yourself
there is no one left but God.
You are all-one
Alone with God!

It happened to Jesus
It can happen to you
If you stay with Jesus
it will happen to you.

Alone
All-one
Alone with God
All-one with God.

Now I understand
why Jesus went out
to the desert hills so often
alone . . .

The only kind of solitude that is fruitful is the solitude that
plunges us into the depths of ourselves to find God. Nikos
Kazantzakis says, "Solitude is fatal to any soul which fails to
burn with a great passion. If, in his solitude, a monk does not
love God to the point of frenzy, he is doomed."[14]

My own experience of solitude proves this true. If the solitude is to be life-giving I must find my way through the laby-
rinth of my distractions right into the heart of God.

I never spoke with God
nor visited in heaven
Yet certain am I of the spot
as if the chart were given.
Emily Dickinson[15]

On some days such a certitude dwells in my heart concerning things of heaven that I can be as confident as Emily. And then there are days when I am plagued with doubts. I am a questioner, Lord. I have never been one to settle down in an armchair with all answers happily tucked inside me. I raise my eyebrows and wonder when I hear people say they never doubt. I confess I am a doubter and on some days I live on a borrowed flame, when mine has gone out. On some days it must be enough for someone else to believe for me.

I doubt, O God, you know I doubt. We've been through all the issues together. From earliest childhood I have been full of question marks and I am not ashamed of them.

Yet somewhere alongside the question marks in my life lives one giant exclamation mark, and it always wins out. I was made for the heights and I feel the urge for climbing. I was also made for the depths. I have a yen to go down into the deep waters where all things are born anew. The heights and the depths! My life seems one great paradox but I've not run from the mystery. I've tasted enough of heaven to believe in it. So on some days I can believe for someone who is living on a borrowed flame.

There are days when I feel as though I've talked with God. I've visited heaven. On those days I understand what the saints mean when they tell us that all the way to heaven is heaven.

With the poet Tagore, I joyfully proclaim, "I have had my invitation to this world's festival, and thus my life has been blessed."[16] Truly, I'm on my way to heaven, and heaven's on the way. No map needed! Just a heart that ever seeks!

It is right always to wait, with a faith energized by Love for the illumination which will enable us to speak. For nothing is so

destitute as a mind philosophizing about God when it is without Him.

The Philokalia[17]

These words touched a chord in my heart today to the extent of inviting tears. My tears accepted the invitation and came slowly, steadily, saltily. They ran down my cheeks until I wondered, Why? Why did these words evoke such feeling in me? I have learned enough about my tears to honor them. They are wiser than I am, especially when they come during prayer. And so I listened. I sat quietly and listened to my tears. I think my tears know something that I need to look at. They know that in spite of all my efforts to open people's hearts to the possibility of deep experience with God, I so often neglect my own daily experience of God. I try to live on the strength of others far too much. I try to glean wisdom from books rather than go through the poverty of being alone with God.

I find it distressing on my spiritual pilgrimage that everyone, including my self, seems so anxious to know what the *experts* are saying about God. I have no quarrel with the giants of the spiritual life. It is wonderful that we have so many people who have faithfully pursued this ache in the human heart, who have searched out its meaning and wrestled with divine things. Yet in my quiet, insightful moments I realize it is not sitting at the feet of the experts that is going to satisfy this ache in my heart. Simone Weil says it so well when she says that all of life is a waiting for God. That brings me back to my utter poverty. My thoughts return to the *Philokalia* and I listen again to these words: "It is right always to wait, with a faith energized by Love for the illumination which will enable us to speak . . ."

All I can do is wait for God. Yet in my loneliness I sometimes need to sit at someone's feet. On some days I would like to come to *you*. I would like to sit at your feet instead of the feet of John of the Cross or Julian of Norwich. I would like to hear of your experience of God, you, little and great, frail and glorious person, you who are living and struggling in this holy and confusing piece of flesh right now, in this day and age, at this moment. I would like to sit at your feet to hear the story of how God comes to you.

Why are we so afraid to trust our own experience of God as valid? Why are we so reluctant to wait in darkness?

It may seem strange for one who is writing a book to confess that the reason it is taking me so long to find the God I am seeking is because I read too much. Yet I know this is true. And that's why the tears came. I find myself philosophizing about my God out of what I have learned from others more than from sitting in darkness waiting for God, and that saddens me.

O Word made Flesh, Sustainer of Life, save me from the emptiness of philosophizing about you only out of the experience of others. Let me trust also the darkness of my own faith that is energized by my love. Even if my waiting in darkness were to be the only truth I ever taste, I would still believe. The ache in me is too deep to take lightly. The illumination that enables me to speak is found only in waiting for you, my God. My tears and my love urge me to wait through the darkest of nights. So I will wait and never be without you.

Prayer fastens the soul to God. . . . When we come to heaven, our prayers shall be waiting for us as part of our delight with endless joyful thanks from God.

Julian of Norwich[18]

I have felt quite fastened to you in prayer lately, my God. I believe it is because I have taken up a different style of praying. I feel more connected and attached to you when I pray because I've given up my own agenda. I use fewer words and so I experience a deeper presence.

What does being fastened to you mean except being united to you? Julian of Norwich and Dom Marmion have taught me so much in prayer. They have been able to lead me to you from within.

I have stopped praying *for* people so much. I try to pray *about* them instead. It is more all-embracing as a means of prayer. It seems that you and I together, Jesus, simply look with love on those we love. It is as though we answer people's prayers *together*. I can see now that the more detached I become, the more you will be able to use me to help answer prayers. It is a lovely way to be used and I feel honored. It is a way of becoming a prayer.

Do you remember yesterday when I felt really desperate and scared? I whispered to you, "Jesus, tell someone in heaven about me." I could swear I heard it thunder. It was as though my name was being announced in heaven. Everyone in heaven seemed to be looking on me with love. I looked back with love. No words! No words! Just love!

My soul felt especially fastened to you at that moment, even though it didn't last long and my distractions soon returned. Still, it was a moment of being in love with you and that one moment was more precious and nourishing than a whole year of words. I know now what Julian means when she says that when I get to heaven I'll find my prayers waiting for me. After all, how could heaven ignore even one look of love?

> One dark night
> fired by love's urgent longing
> ah, the sheer grace—
> I went out unseen,
> my house being now all stilled
> . . . with no other light or guide
> than the one that burned in my heart.
> This guided me
> more surely than the light of noon
> to where he waited for me
> him I knew so well.
> *John of the Cross*[19]

When it is so dark that there is no other light to guide me save the one that burns in my heart, then it is dark indeed. Yet this is the light in which I have come to trust. It is a light that I feel rather than see. It is an ache in my heart that yearns for union with the beloved. Like John of the Cross I am constantly fired by love's urgent longing. Unlike John, I am unable to get my house all stilled. Alas, a hushed house I do not own. My

house seems more like a noisy little cage. A cage? Yes, because
something beautiful is imprisoned there. It is the self I refuse
to embrace, the self I won't allow to be united to the beloved.
That self is imprisoned.

There is hope in this noisy little cage, though, for I am not
one who is satisfied with my imprisonment. I have come to the
conclusion that there is no way to free myself. You, O God,
must set me free and I must allow you the space to move freely
in my life. I am not content with myself as I am. Love's urgent
longing presses me on. I want to be all I can be. I want to give
up all of my self that I don't need to be myself. If I do that, will
there be nothing left but you, my God? Will I then be no one?
How frightening to be no one! At this point in my musing I
have questions as to whether I am still Christian in my thought.
If Jesus took on my humanity, then my humanness must be
good. Surely I am not to disappear myself.

This is my dilemma. I am attracted to a spirituality that is
negating: an emptying and forgetting of self, a total surrender,
an abandonment, a seed-falling-to-the-ground-and-dying kind
of experience. Yet at the same time I am attracted to an incarnational spirituality: finding God fleshed out in everything, embracing all as good, celebrating, loving, living, and cherishing
life, leaving the blessing of myself, in Christ, everywhere I go,
finding heaven at my fingertips.

In many ways these two spiritualities seem to be opposites,
yet there is a connection. Incarnational spirituality encourages
me to take my false self to the Divine Heart with eyes wide
open. Since nothing but good can fit in the heart of God, my
false self will have to get lost somewhere between God and me,
between heaven and earth. Perhaps, after all, this is a more
exciting way of losing myself, to take my entire self to the heart
of God, knowing that what is pure will remain. Nothing is
really lost. It is only converted. When my false self stops lying,
it is no longer false. It becomes flesh again in a new creation.

It all seems such a paradox, and my strong feelings to die
and live create some confusion. My love's urgent longing tells
me to let go, to let this mysterious unnamed ache be my guide

and lead me into the arms of God, blind and unseeing, yet trusting. My love's urgent longing also tells me to stand tall with eyes wide open, to embrace everything as gift, as part of the Word made Flesh, and let it lead me into the heart of God, all-seeing and aware. I feel the pull. I love and live the paradox. My Christian monastic way of life is an emptying and a filling, a deep blindness and a deep seeing, a Good Friday and an Easter Sunday.

My restless, questioning spirit used to envy the calm, laid-back type of person. How I longed for quiet assurance! How I longed to be docile and unquestioning! This evening I feel more content with my restless heart, for I know that Christ lives there. Unhushed though my house is, Christ lives there in my love's urgent longing. When the time is right he will calm this storm.

. . . the mama did send me in a hurry to the wood-shed. It was for two loads of wood she wanted. I did bring in the first load in a hurry. The second load I brought not so. I did pick up all the sticks my arms could hold. While I was picking them up, I looked long looks at them. I went not to the kitchen with them in a quick way. I was meditating. I did have thinks about the tree they all were before they got chopped up. I did wonder how I would feel if I was a very little piece of wood that got chopped out of a big tree. I did think that it would have hurt my feelings. I felt the feelings of the wood. They did have a very sad feel.

Just when I was getting that topmost stick a bit wet with sympathy tears—then the mama did come up behind me with a switch. She said while she did switch, "Stop your meditations," and while she did switch, I did drop the wood. I felt the feels the sticks of wood felt when they hit the floor. Then I did pick them up with care and I put them all in the wood-box back of the cook stove. . . . But all the time I was churning (the butter) I did hum a little song. It was a good-bye song to the sticks in the wood-box back of the kitchen stove.

When the churning was done and the butter was come, the mama did lift all the little lumps of butter out of the churn. Then she did pat them together in a big lump, and this she put away in the butter-box in the wood-shed. When she went to lay herself down to rest on the bed, she did call me to rub her head. I like to rub the mama's

head, for it does help the worry lines to go away. Often I rub her head, for it is often she does have longings to have it so. And I do think it is very nice to help people have what they do have longings for.

Opal Whiteley[20]

One of my dearest friends introduced me to Opal with these words: "I think you are Opal, returned to life." It is the greatest compliment I have ever received, yet I am unworthy to claim such honor, for my life holds far too much selfishness to be compared to Opal's. She was an incredible child. She fits G. K. Chesterton's definition of a saint: one who exaggerates what the world neglects.[21]

I think an Opal lives in each of us. It is that part of us that is truly present, all-seeing, in constant awe, ever forgiving, still child enough to be amazed and in love. Most of us have sadly neglected that part of us. We lost it somewhere between the ages of twelve and thirty-three. Jesus exaggerated the Opal part of himself between the ages of twelve and thirty-three, but we seem to lose it then. The Opal part of us does still exist. If only we can get it to live rather than just exist. If only we can believe in it and renew it, the world will be a better place to live.

As I pray the journal of this foster child who lived in nine lumber camps in Oregon before she reached the age of twelve, I am in awe of her tremendous sensitivity and creativity. I am also saddened at how much she was misunderstood by the adults she lived with.

She has become for me a spiritual mentor. There is a plaque on my wall bearing the simple name Opal. Her name has become a prayer in my life. I pray it especially on days when I feel swallowed up in self-centeredness, for she was so totally other-centered. In her childlike simplicity she walked through life exaggerating what grown-ups neglect. And like so many saints, she was misunderstood for her vision.

Opal, my sister and my guide, I am looking for that part of myself that is all love. I am looking for that part of myself that is all presence. I am looking for that part of myself that is all understanding. I am looking for that part of myself that is all wonder.

Opal, the whole world is longing with me for love, presence, understanding, and wonder. I, too, think it is very nice to help people have what they do have longings for. The sadness, Opal, is that they do not understand what it is they are having longings for. Look long looks at all the people who are so yearning. Let your sympathy tears fall upon hearts that are splintered like the little pieces of wood cut from the big tree. Sing a little song to the heart pieces as you did to the wood pieces, but let it not be a good-bye song. Let it be a healing song so that the broken hearts can have what it is they are truly longing for.

Ask Jesus to send people to this world who will have the courage to exaggerate what the world neglects. Opal, I am asking for saints. Send saints! Send folks who are willing to bear the misunderstanding that it takes to be a saint. And finally, ask Jesus to rub the forehead of the world so that our worry lines will go away and trust lines will come upon us. For Jesus, too, does think that it is nice to help folks have what they do have longings for.

8. Finding God in the Mailbox

You used to write us little enough, but now you do not write even that little; and if your brevity keeps increasing with time, it seems likely to become complete speechlessness. Therefore return to your old custom, for I shall never again find fault with you for practicing Laconic brevity on me by letter. Nay, even your little letters, seeing that they are tokens of magnanimity, I shall value highly. Only write to me.

Saint Basil the Great to Olympius[1]

Letters are the stories of our souls. Unlike a telephone call, a letter can be picked up again and again. It can be deeply pondered. It can be eaten. Always serve letters with a cup of tea and a footstool. Celebrate "the reading" slowly. It is irreverent to read a letter fast.

I treasure my letters like early morning sunrises. I see the rays between the lines. I hear the dreams and yearnings, the gratitude and the delight. I hear the questions and the musings, all coming from the heart of this newly published author. A letter bears its own copyright. Standing before my mailbox holding an original very limited edition in my hands is like standing before a feast.

From ancient times, letters have been sources of inspiration, teaching, and soul-baring. In the charming letter from Basil the Great quoted above, both humor and human longing can be seen. Here is Basil, that great Cappadocian father, scholar, and ascetic, begging for the consolation that a letter can bring. His words are truly a glimpse into the humanity of the saints.

The spiritual letters of John Chapman are filled with wonderful pieces of advice to those who are seeking spiritual growth. One of my favorites is written to someone to whom he suspects he has given incorrect advice. In this letter a humble owning of his fallibility along with a claiming of new wisdom is seen.

I have come to the conclusion that one can remain united to God even when one goes to sleep in time of prayer. Don't laugh. I say this, because I think I told you that, when one feels one is going to sleep, it is good to try and think some good thoughts, or even reason out something, in order to keep awake. If I said so, I was wrong. I see that it simply stops prayer dead; so that thinking is more disastrous than sleep![2]

I am pleased with this delightful piece of advice. I agree that we take ourselves too seriously when we try to think our sleep away. Even the Psalms say that God provides for the beloved while they are asleep (Ps. 127:2).

Any piece of advice that tells me not to depend too much on my own words or thoughts is food for my soul. Abbot Marmion gives similar advice in one of his spiritual letters when he says,

When you feel invited to remain in silence at our Lord's feet like Magdalen just looking at him with your heart, without saying anything, don't cast about for any thoughts or reasonings but just remain in loving adoration . . . if he invites you to beg, beg; if to be silent, remain silent; if to show your misery to God, just do so. Let him play on the fibres of your heart like a harpist, and draw forth the melody he wishes.[3]

Sometimes letters are cries from the heart as we explain to our friends the burdens of life, the inconsistencies, the infinite sadness that has come upon us. Etty Hillesum writes such a letter to her friend Tide from Westerbork. She is describing a little hunchback Russian woman in the concentration camp.

She stands there in front of me, a green silk kimono wrapped round her small, misshapen figure. She has the very wise, bright eyes of a child. She looks at me for a long time in silence, searchingly, and then says, "I would like, oh, I really would like to be able to swim away in my tears." . . . She asks me with her strange accent in the voice of a child that begs for forgiveness. "Surely God will be able to understand my doubts in a world like this, won't He?" Then she turns away from me in an almost loving gesture of infinite sadness, and throughout the night I see the misshapen, green, silk-clad figure moving between beds, doing small services for those about to depart.[4]

This portion of Etty's letter spent several poignant weeks with me. You never know just how a letter is going to feed you. It may feed you the sorrow that makes you want to turn away from your own shallow living. It may feed you the wisdom that leads you to explore new depths to which you are being called. It may feed you delight that helps you revel in the memory of a cherished friend. It may feed you encouragement, asking your heart to leap to new heights.

It has long been a custom of mine to pray with the letters I receive. Sometimes I sit quietly holding the memory of the sender in my heart. Jesus and I look on the author of the letter with love. At times I use a single phrase from a letter as my prayer-mantra throughout the day. Quite often I enter choice portions of a letter into my journal. My journaling with the letter sometimes becomes an actual answer to the letter and at other times simply remains a prayer in my journal.

In this Chapter I share from my journal pieces of letters from friends and my prayer responses to them. I've chosen to use the letter format here for my responses even if my journal entries were not always sent as letters. These selections are indeed testimonies to the truth that God can be found in the mailbox.

There was a time when I tried to do everything right and proper. That seemed to be my goal. But suddenly all I want is to be holy. I long so for a deep holiness.

(Klara)

Klara, dear sister,

So you want to be a saint! What joy to hear a sister of mine so yearning. I am with you in the yearning and yet it is such a dangerous yearning. If we become holy, meaning whole and mature in Christ, the effects of our holiness will be felt in Rome,

Washington, Fort Smith, and beyond, for we will be impelled to speak out against injustice. Do you still want to be holy?

I blush at my silence in the face of so much injustice in our world. Every time I get this fierce longing, rather like you expressed in your letter, I see the cross off in the distance and I step back a bit. How can I say that I want to be a saint, yet want so little to do with the cross?

Chesterton's definition of a saint lies on my heart again. What a challenge! A saint is one who exaggerates what the world neglects. If I could choose one great gift that the world is neglecting I would have to choose feminine energy. It is what we need to save the world. It is what we need to be saints. Feminine energy is powerful because it is pure presence— gentle yet firm. It is an energy that gives warmth, comfort, and spirit simply by its presence. It receives rather than takes. It invites rather than demands. It unfolds rather than controls. It empowers rather than overpowers. It finds itself in being rather than in doing. Feminine energy shows her best face in leisure. She doesn't *take* time. She *has* time. She has time to *be*. The world is starving for this energy. It is part of the fire Christ came to cast on the earth—a slow flame that burns from within and gradually transforms what it touches, precisely because it touches rather than clutches.

Today a small possibility for that transformation crept into the cell of my heart. It came in the word *leisure*. Each day I have been choosing a word that I pray will become flesh in me. Today my word is *leisure*. David Steindl-Rast says that leisure is taking things separate, one by one, and singling them out for grateful consideration.[5] He is saying the same thing that Opal is saying when she has "long looks" at things. What wonderful teachers God sends me! A monk and a little girl! God can use anyone to continue the work of creation. All God needs is some flesh and a single heart. So today I'm taking things to my heart, one by one. I'm singling them out for grateful consideration. David also says that whenever you single out something or someone for grateful consideration you have a little celebration. What a delightful thought!

These were my little celebrations for today: the giant saguaro outside my window, the cooing of the mourning dove, the roadrunner, the memory of my community, my morning coffee, the desert hills surrounding my hermitage, and the dog's excited leap as I took her for a morning walk.

These little momentary celebrations may be the very secret of holiness. I admit it is easier to be present when deadlines aren't upon me, but even in the desert I falter. I miss the crumbs for wanting the loaf. Do you want to be holy, Klara? Slow down. Take long looks at everything. Single many things out for grateful consideration.

Macrina

Stop analyzing the mystery, just sit at Jesus' feet!
(Ever-Seeking)

Dear Ever-Seeking,

Your letter could be ranked in the files of the saints. I have been reading the spiritual letters of Marmion and he gives me the same advice as you have given: don't get so bogged down in words and thoughts, questioning and analyzing, that you can't taste the mystery.

You know me well and you are right. I have been steeped in trying to understand the mystery of the Eucharist. Understanding has often been a block for me. I want to understand. Yet there is so much I cannot understand, especially when I get into the realm of mystery.

I hear you and God saying to me, "Stop trying to understand the mystery. Just look at it. Revere it and be in it." In some small way are we not all entwined in this great mystery of the Eucharist? Are we not all meant to be bread and wine?

Is not divinity hidden in our own frail body and blood? Is not divinity hidden in humanity?

Thank you for your words of wisdom. I will try to stop analyzing the mystery. I will simply look at it with long, grateful looks. I will sit at Jesus' feet. I will sit at your feet, too.

From your sister who has tasted the mystery,
Macrina

. . . to walk with less hurry inside.

(Joyce)

Joyce,

Your words are like ointment for my soul. My days have been filled with hurry. I hurry on the inside. I hurry on the outside. Then I give talks on slowing down. I would feel like an utter hypocrite but for the fact that I can talk most passionately about that which I feel the greatest lack. I understand experientially what hurrying does to the soul. I am beginning to see what violence I do to myself when I hurry.

When I prayed your words, my deep self got immensely excited, hoping, I suppose, that relief was on the way. My poor deep self has had a hard time of it lately. I drag it around with me in my haste. It has no choice but to go where I go and at my pace. That part of me that was made to adore has been enslaved in my busyness. It is crying for freedom. It is crying for the space to stand and stare. It is crying for something slow and something quiet.

Today I knew I must be obedient to its cry. I fixed myself a cup of tea and sat down in the middle of the day. Can you believe it? In the middle of the day! And it wasn't even Sunday! What a victory! My inner self nestled up within and tried to give me a hug. My quiet smiled on my noise, my slow smiled on my hurry. Musing on this calming moment, I received these words:

the quiet in me smiled on my noise
the slow in me smiled on my hurry
and my life miracled into
a calm on the lake.

Jesus woke up in my boat
without my asking
and commanded the winds
to subside.

I was asked not to run away
from my noise and my hurry
but to enter it
and embrace it most gently.

it was at the moment
of my entering
that I felt the miracle.

the quiet in me smiled on my noise
the slow in me smiled on my hurry
and my life miracled into
a calm on the lake.

It is truly a miracle what happens in my life when I let God
have me. I have never felt very docile, yet I have my moments,
and today is one of them, when I think I could hand over anything God would ask for. I know myself well enough not to say
that too loudly, but the yearning is here. Perhaps this is the
reason I run so much. A part of me is terrified of what I will
hear in stillness.

> From your partially slowed-down friend,
> Macrina

**This card made me think of you: the unicorn amidst the spears.
Still, to be hunted by God is not to die, but to fall in love. Hard,
when Jesus is asleep in your boat.** *(Nicholas)*

Nicholas,

I hear you in the deep places of my soul. It is hard to understand the spears. They do not seem like darts of love when I am running from them, and yet there is something mysteriously loving about them. The spears are nothing less than the glances of God. They slice through my being and I am both wounded and healed.

On some days I am at a loss to understand why God keeps hunting me. I have slipped from the spears of that loving glance so many times. I have even slipped from the divine embrace. I suppose after that long spell of hiding, my vulnerability attracts God. The beloved long-suffering hunter sees me on the verge of surrendering, sees that I am almost ready to let him in. He rests a moment from the exhaustion that any lover feels. He rests, and I think he is asleep in my boat. While he sleeps he waits for me to cry out for mercy. He waits for me to become the huntress, to throw to him the spears of my glances.

Speaking of hunting, have you read *Medicine Woman* by Lynn Andrews? Such a wonderful story, especially if you are searching for the feminine power within, and most of the world, both men and women, would do well to search. Lynn is an apprentice of Agnes Whistling Elk, a medicine woman. At one point Agnes is teaching Lynn to be a huntress. Lynn is amazed at Agnes's ability to see. She asks Agnes, "How can you see like that?" The medicine woman's answer to Lynn would do well to settle in my heart for a stay. "I know where to look," Agnes claims. "Develop hungry eyes—eyes that get hungry before your stomach."[6] Ah! I think I would like such eyes.

Nicholas, let's do it. Let's develop eyes and hearts that are hungrier than our stomachs. Let's pray for eyes and hearts that will not dodge the loving spears of God's glance. You are right. Truly, to be hunted by God is not to die but to fall in love.

I have fallen. I have fallen in love. And the best way to describe it is to remember King Arthur when he drank from the Holy Grail and was revived. His words from the movie *Ex-caliber* linger in my heart: "I never knew how empty my soul was until it was filled." Surely this must be the cry of anyone who has been hunted by God, and found. "I never knew how empty my soul was until it was filled." This is my cry as the glance of God finds me.

Fondly, from the unicorn amidst spears,
Macrina

Part of the call I sensed so strongly during my retreat is to be humble, poor, and full of love. It seems to be the perfect ointment for me, for our community and beyond. . . . I would say no to this call but I cannot for it seems the call has chosen me. Hammarskjöld says, "Weep, weep if you can but don't complain. The way chose you and you must be grateful." I feel grateful and I feel chosen. Do pray that I can be humble, poor, and full of love.

(Mary)

Mary, my sister,

What a joy to be in communion with you, and oh, to feel it so across the miles. Your call is my call! I, too, feel chosen and grateful. What wonderful ointment for us all: to be humble, poor, and full of love. Yes, I am sure if we could wear these holy cloaks, everyone we contacted would feel the anointing. I promise not to complain that the way has chosen me, and on occasion I will weep.

God has had a hidden face lately. I am truly in a "cloud of unknowing." It is all such a mystery. I can't pray and yet I feel so much peace.

I think Opal will be my spiritual director this year. I hear her saying, "I have longings for more eyes. There is much to see in this world all about."[7] How I wish that more eyes was the only thing I longed for. I feel myself still wanting so much that does not lead me to union with God.

This morning I decided to pray with Opal's "long looks." It dawned on me that the long looks she was so engaged in were nothing less than real presence. She knew how to look at life deeply. What wisdom to learn from a child! I decided to begin my day by celebrating real presence with long looks. These celebrations have lingered throughout the day. It has been a good prayer.

My first long look of the day was to watch the dawn come over the hills silhouetting the saguaro community in its background. I just looked and loved it in silence. Having coffee with it was my second celebration. I had long looks at the steam from my coffee rising like incense. Then came Morning Praise and Eucharist with my new family. I had long loving looks at the folks who will slowly become my community. There were many little celebrations in between, but one I take special note of was watching the quail pass by my window in procession. It's so precious how they follow each other so reverently. They would make wonderful Catholics the way they love processions, only it would be difficult to train them to carry candles. But perhaps the little antenna that they carry so proudly on top of their heads is all the candle they need. Enough of quail processions through the desert! I'm back to yearning for God. How I pray that all the yeast in me will be changed into fresh bread this year so that I can return with more of myself to break among my sisters and beyond!

I could hardly believe it when you said you needed to overcome your laziness and that it isn't just procrastination. I had just dealt with that very subject in my journal. I also have problems with laziness, in case you haven't noticed. Anyway, back to my journal—my prayer-mantra for the day was, "I have pondered over my ways and returned to your will" (Ps. 119:59 Grail). When I started pondering over my ways it turned out to be quite a list. I will certainly not include my entire list. On the list, however, I included laziness. In parentheses beside it I wrote: "I like to soften it by calling it procrastination—sounds less sinful." Well, today when I was reading in the *Philokalia* I found a wonderful passage that can nourish us both.[8] This is taken from a letter written to Nicolas the Solitary by Saint Mark the Ascetic. Mark says to descend into the depths of the heart and search out three powerful giants of the Devil: (1) ignorance, the source of all evils; (2) forgetfulness, its close relation and helper; and (3) laziness, which weaves the dark shroud enveloping the soul in murk. I know this third vice sounds awful. He says that it supports and strengthens the other two, consolidating them so that evil becomes deep-rooted and persistent in the negligent soul.

Mark says that through strict attention and control of the intellect, as well as help from Above, we will be able to track down these evil passions about which most people are ignorant. Now, Mary, don't lose heart, because here's the way to do it. You and I need to take up the weapons of righteousness that are directly opposed to these evils. And these are (1) mindfulness of God, the cause of all blessings; (2) the light of spiritual knowledge, through which the soul awakens from its slumbers; and (3) true ardor, which makes the soul eager for salvation. Only careful attention and deep prayer can help us to acquire these virtues. But when real knowledge, mindfulness of God's word, and true ardor have set up their tents in our heart, those three enemies are supposed to move out.

I have a little difficulty with the word ardor. It just doesn't exist in my vocabulary, but for Mark the Ascetic I suppose it was a household word. However, when I reflect on its meaning it does seem a wonderful means to drive out enemies of the spiritual life. I end up saying, Oh for the gift of true ardor! Translated that would be: burning zeal, fire, flames, warmth of emotion, love, passion for good, conviction. Mary, with all those bright good spirits moving around in us, our laziness has got to take flight. Mark the Ascetic is right and Nicolas was blessed to have such a spiritual friend.

You must forgive this letter. I had thought it was to be the light and friendly kind, but out here in the desert when one gets in her cell, you just don't know what might take place in the soul if you give it a chance.

Mary, the daily discipline of listening and responding to meaning in life is what David Steindl-Rast calls obedience. And according to Teresa of Avila, obedience is what there must be *some* of around if we are to be able to call ourselves monks or nuns. Surely somewhere in the world there must be one truly obedient person, one who daily listens and responds to meaning. For that person I give thanks. And for the yearning in our own hearts I also give thanks. I wish you the "good zeal" that Benedict talks about in our rule.

> I feel grateful that *the way* has chosen me,
> Macrina

I am almost brought to tears when I think of what God has happened between us.

> *(Rachel)*

Rachel,

I have been praying with this line from your letter for several days now. I, too, am in awe of the healing wings that have hovered over us, drawing us back into the circle of friendship. It feels like a great mending. It is a mending. God has been here all the while knitting us together again, urging us to look at all the good that is ours in Christ. And we have both looked. Thanks to each of us for looking.

We took our wounds with us when we parted and we wore them like badges for a while. But even wounds get stale. Fresh wounds have urged me not to stack wound upon wound. So I started praying with my wounds.

About my own part in this wound I have to say that it was partially a decision to let it go, and yet it was so much deeper than a decision. It was more like a cooperation with grace. It was not so much that I was doing something about the wound, but more like I was allowing something to be done in me. I think it is quite possible to pray for healing and not really want it. I am happy to say, stubborn and willful as I am, this time I really wanted the healing.

Part of the beauty of coming through this wound with you is that we have recognized ourselves as pilgrims. Being a pilgrim is living through the tension between who we are and who we yearn to be. It is especially healing to know that we have not just forgiven each other but that we even cherish and honor each other.

And yes, it is God who has happened between us. It is the very flesh of God. It is Jesus. It seems that there is no end to the number of times that the Word can become flesh in our lives.

I cherish your friendship,
Macrina

I live a lot on memories. . . . at a distance I think friendships hibernate. I don't think they die.

(Nicholas)

Nicholas,

Praying with your letter was like a treasure house of memories opening up before me. I had to be careful not to let the memories overwhelm me. One at a time is all I can digest. They are so rich. Rich, because life is rich.

Today then, thanks to you, I prayed with memories. One by one I cherished them and gathered them up as crumbs. It was nourishment that I would never have dreamed possible. It is such a grace to be able to reflect prayerfully on one's past experiences.

It is not easy to be truly present to each life event while it is happening. That's why it is so valuable to go back to the memory when we are a bit wiser and more detached from the event. We can read between the lines and the words of the experience better after we have distanced ourselves from it. We can be more objective and more fair, and even more present. You have always been better in reading between the lines than I have, but I am happy to report I am learning.

It occurred to me in prayer today what a tremendous gift it is to give myself this special blessing of praying with my memories. God came today in my mailbox and reminded me that friendships do not die. They simply wait awhile. They quietly remember. In the absence of the beloved they age like good wine.

I am happy to say, in spite of the distance and the infrequent letters, you are good wine in my life, always willing to be poured out again when the sacred moment returns. What more can I add except the wisdom of Opal—it's such a comfort to have a friend when "lonesome feels" do come.

Macrina

. . . **acceptance rather than expectations.**

(Bernie)

Bernie,

Those four words stood out in your letter. They visited my heart, so I decided to stay with them for a while. I have had such an overwhelming desire to love others just as they are. Acceptance is such a beautiful word. How I long for it to become flesh in my life. I am so full of expectations: expectations for myself, for others, and even, at times, for God. I have our agenda all planned out, and how disappointed I allow myself to be when we don't measure up to my expectations!

I think of the rich young man who came running up to Jesus. He was so full of zeal. He had a burning desire to be a disciple. But when he heard the cost, he walked away sad. I will never forget the look of love Jesus gave when he saw him coming. I have no doubt that when our nameless young man walked away sad, Jesus' look of love followed him. Acceptance rather than expectations! Jesus had an incredible ability to love people where they were. He didn't demand that they change on the spot.

I have adopted Jesus' look of love as a way of prayer. When I find my expectations rising to the demanding point, I simply look at the person with whom I am in conflict. I use the look of Jesus as my prayer. I whisper quietly, "And Jesus looked on him with love. And Jesus looked on her with love." Then I look on him or her with love. That look of love almost always brings comfort, and I find myself filling up with acceptance rather than expectations.

There is another person we both know who lived the philosophy of acceptance rather than expectations. Her name is Opal. I think back to that evening she was sent away from the dinner table for a remark that was meant to be all kindness. In her place of exile she wrote:

I have wonders about folks. They are hard to understand. I think I will just say a little prayer. My, I do have such hungry feels now. They at the table are not through yet. I make swallows down my throat. It is most hard not to eat what I have saved for my animal friends. But they will like it—so I can wait waits until breakfast time. I can. In-between times I will have thinks and prayers.[9]

Perhaps we would all have more acceptance if we put ourselves in the corner once in a while for "thinks" and for "prayers."

I am having "thinks" about your acceptance of me this evening. It is such a mystery of love. We think so differently about things. I am sure I must sound quite heretical to you at times. And yet, you do more than tolerate my ways. You accept me with a tenderness that I find healing. Truly, it is acceptance rather than expectations that I feel. If you do that for me, I am confident you can do it for others.

And speaking of being heretical, do you know that when I was a child I used to pray for the Devil? I just couldn't imagine God not loving the Devil. I had a strong hunch that one day even the Devil would fall down in adoration before God. In my child's heart I knew it would happen and I felt special knowing that with my prayers I was helping with the Devil's conversion.

Can you imagine my surprise, then, long after I was given the name Macrina at my monastic profession, to discover that Saint Macrina held such a belief. She, along with many of the holy ones of the Eastern church, believed that the day would come when all things would be under Jesus' feet and even the devils would fall down in worship. So if you're going in for heresies, that might not be a bad one to hold. A heresy, some-one has said, is just a truth pushed too far. My question is, How far is too far? And who decides?

Can we accept the heresy of God's extravagant love? Or do we have a God who is putting people in the electric chair? Do we have a God who is always probing and condemning? Do we have a God who excommunicates people for thinking?

Since we are on the topic of terrible judgments, I do not have it in my heart to imagine that our God would ever say to anyone, *Anathama sit* (Let it be condemned)!

Perhaps my child's wisdom was not so very foolish after all. Acceptance rather than expectations! Can we accept the accept-ance of God? Or do our expectations demand that God must not be merciful?

With love,
Macrina

I am in such anguish. I feel such a strong call to simplify my life but I cannot. Everywhere I compromise. I would be embarrassed to tell you some of the foolish things I have bought lately. It seems there is this big hole in me and I keep trying to fill it full of the craziest things but the more I put in, the emptier I feel.

(Felicia)

Felicia, soul-sister,

I have one of those holes in my life, too. Could the secret that we have not yet learned be that the more we take out, the fuller we get? Just wondering!

Your letter was timely, for I am wrestling with the same thing. Your anguish made my prayer all the richer, for it is also my anguish. The more I yearn to be poor and empty, the more I see my cluttered home and my divided heart. It is not a pretty sight.

I can offer you two little treasures from the wisdom of oth-ers. They may not console you, but I think they will confirm that you are on the right path in your search.

The first treasure is from a book I am reading called *Peace Pilgrim*, which has this to say about the very thing we are struggling with:

I am not a slave to comfort and convenience. I wouldn't be a pilgrim if I were. We can allow false beliefs to govern our lives and be enslaved by them. Most people do not wish to be free. They would prefer to moan and chafe about how impossible it is to give up their various enslavements to possessions, food, drink, smoking, and so forth. It is not that they can't give them up—they don't really want to give them up.[10]

My heart did not sing when I read that passage. I did not particularly like the message, but I needed it and so felt blessed by it. When I read that most people do not really want to be free, I blushed before God. For me, it is true. I do and I don't. It's that terrible pull that Paul talks about in Romans. I fail to carry out the things I want to do, and I find myself doing the very things I hate (Rom. 7:15).

I think what is important here is that we are engaged in honest self-criticism, that we are willing to keep looking for the good in us that really wants to surrender to God. The grace to surrender is not beyond our reach.

For me, this call to simplicity feels right even though I haven't yet found the strength of spirit to make it a reality in my life. It seems like a call to a way of life that I *must* find the courage to live. My friend Mary reminds me that it is not a way I have chosen. The way has chosen me. And I must be grateful. I must not turn back.

This brings me to the second treasure I want to share with you. It is when Paul says to the Corinthians, "It is you I want, not your possessions" (2 Cor. 12:14). That was a powerful statement for me. When I read it, I tried to imagine Christ saying to me, "It is you I want, not your possessions."

If I wanted to rationalize my call to simplicity, I suppose I could say that this call to get rid of possessions is not the heart of the matter; what God wants is *me*. And this is true. However, that could be an escape preventing me from honestly looking at what enslaves me. Of course, the treasured possession God wants is *me*. I could give up everything and still be full of myself or proud of my great emptiness. Still, the giving up of clutter is a valid symbol. It can be the beginning of letting go, and so the beginning of truly giving myself. But it is important to remember the reason for taking inventory of my life. Surely it is so that I can have a freer self to present to God.

One last comment. Don't worry about being embarrassed over the compromises you make on your journey. I am with you in that, too. You are aware that in a recent attempt to limit my wardrobe I designed a simple monastic habit. I guess you might say it is a monk's dress, containing a cowl rather than a veil. It has become my attire here at my monastery and for some professional functions. My second habit is a blue-jean skirt. Since I am basically a latent hippie, I feel pretty comfortable with this style of dress, though there are some in my community and elsewhere who think it is a step backward. However, I am content in this regard, for I am much less concerned about approval than I used to be. That in itself, in my opinion, is a step forward.

The amusing part of this is that one day I looked at myself and came to the conclusion that my earrings just didn't fit with this monk's garb. I have never cared much for jewelry but for some strange reason have had a yen for earrings. Reluctantly I took them off and put them away. Please note, I said *put them away* rather than *gave them away*. Don't laugh, but periodically I find myself putting them on again, because you see, the truth is: I really don't want the holes in my ears to grow shut. That doesn't sound very detached, does it? This would seem silly to many people. I realize that earrings are not sinful, but the call in my life goes far beyond merely trying to avoid sin. The earrings are symbolic of the many things I still cling to. I compromise a lot, too. If I recall correctly, somewhere in his writings Meister Eckhart says that it is where clinging to things ends, that God begins to be. May we be able to let go to the extent that God will be more fully in our lives.

From your still-clinging friend,
Macrina

Whenever I get lonesome, I look into my heart. I can always find you hanging out there—reading a poem, or saying a prayer or rustling through the leaves in the cemetery or giving a homily or drinking a beer, or a glass of wine or cup of tea. . . . Do you remember the healing ceremony we had at St. Thomas? I have never forgotten it. Sometimes when I'm feeling sad, or just downright despondent, I think of Father (what was his name?) placing his hands upon my head and blessing me. It always helps. Always. You are right about memories. Letters help heal us too.

(Debra)

Debra,

Today my prayer consisted in simply going to my heart and re-membering all the folks I've stored there. It is not cold storage. It is a quite warm and tender place.

I saw all the people who have been a significant part of my life but with whom I've not had time for the luxury of steady correspondence. I sat in silence and just looked on all these dear ones with fondness. In my mind's eye they filed by in slow procession like the quail in the desert, one by one. I prayed each person and looked on each with love.

There were college students from campus ministry days. There were people from the various church ministries in which I've worked. There were those who have made retreats at our Center. There was my family and my classmates. I saw the symbols that once bound us together and I praised God for this unexpected communion that came to me because of your letter.

Your own name then became a prayer in my heart and I heard again the crunch of leaves as we waded through leftover autumn, reading Robert Frost. I saw us stuck in the sand on the Arkansas River. I visualized again the glass of wine shared in friendship and saw the steam rising from our teacups. It was a good prayer, but best of all was my memory that we could have a celebration on a crust of bread and a glass of water. Do you remember? It was poetry we ate. Dorothy Day says that even a crust is a banquet with companionship. And I would say that even poetry is a banquet with companionship. Beautiful memories!

Tonight as I pray this letter, what touches me most is your unique memory of the healing service. I say *unique* because even though you cannot remember the name of the one who blessed you that night, you remember the healing that took place, and that is as it should be. I find that awesome. You remember the touch of hands. We are a people who like to have our names remembered. Perhaps, after all, there is something deeper than our names that must live on. What is most important to remember? The name of the servant who was used as an instrument for healing? Or the very act of healing? We both know the answer. Thanks for a lovely insight. I will remember.

Jesus, make of us your servants. Use us in your ministry of healing. Let our names be forgotten. But may the healing live on.

Macrina

The plight of some of our theologians and church leaders pains me. Sometimes I fear we are going through another Inquisition in the church.

(Judy)

Judy,

Yes, it is a dilemma. So many people in the church are getting the ax today, and it seems to be the sensitive and compassionate ones—the ones who aren't afraid to ask questions and explore, those who are more comfortable with a church in process than a church in stone.

Sometimes I think Rome honors the dead saints and persecutes the live ones. I guess, in a way, it has always been like that. I keep hoping the church will learn from experience. Past experience, however, does not teach us unless we reflect on it. How much reflection Rome does, I don't know. Last night I kept vigil for people in high places. I prayed that those in our church hierarchy will be given the wisdom to reflect prayerfully on our past experience so that all concerned can have the greening of new growth. I prayed to Galileo, Teilhard de Chardin and all those wounded saints whose wisdom was not recognized until they died.

I do worry about Rome more than I say aloud. Something is not right there and yet something is very right about the Catholic church for me. Sometimes I get so scared. It feels like Rome is leaving the Catholic church, that simple, sacramental church. The church of the "little ones" has turned into the church of the big and powerful ones. I want to cry out to those men, "Don't leave," but they would never understand what I mean. It is such a helpless feeling.

But then there are times when I am quite proud of Rome. I browse through the encyclicals and pastoral statements and find quite a prophetic voice there. The church seems so on target in areas of peace and justice. Of course, I'm aware that justice for women in church ministry is not included. That is a tragic flaw. I do pray that God will mend our tragic flaws.

My gut feeling is that we must stand by the church in her vision and in her blindness. Yet we must never forget that we have as much responsibility to challenge our church leaders as they have to challenge us. We must not forget the prophets in the pews. They have been ignored far too long.

From one of the "little ones,"
Macrina

Sometimes I think I can only claim to be "Christian." When one breaks it down any more than that I begin to waver and can't make a

clear choice. Even the *Bhagavad Gita* has a place in my heart. Am I a
fence sitter or a lost sheep?

(Reid)

Dear Reid,

A fence sitter? I hardly think so. A lost sheep? Definitely
not! You are a seeker. I am too. I've chosen to be a seeker within
a particular denomination. At this time in your life you are
seeking within what Simone Weil calls "the paste of common
humanity." Simone felt that she had a vocation to remain anonymous. Yet she never stopped seeking.

Perhaps the opposite of a seeker is a settler. There are people who settle in. In churches they often become pew warmers.
I'm speaking of people who aren't there for any kind of passionate reasons of their own. Sometimes they are there because
they inherited a certain church from their ancestors. Or they
may be there because it is socially acceptable to belong to a
church. Sometimes people belong to a church because they are
afraid. It takes a great deal of conversion and a lot of dwelling
in God to be in love rather than in fear.

I like the story about the man who, while walking down a
country road, meets an angel. The angel is carrying in one hand
a bucket of water. In the other hand she carries a flaming torch.
When the man inquires of the angel what she is about, the
angel answers, "With this water I'm going to quench all the
fires of hell and with the torch I am going to burn down all the
mansions of heaven; and then we're going to find out who *really*
loves God."

A wonderful story! It should be told in churches the world
over. Far too often we settle down in our church pews because
we fear the great punishment, or we long for the great reward.
For people who are created in God's image, it would seem more
appropriate to be there because we are in love. Perhaps we
don't spend enough time dwelling in God to fall in love with
God.

In addition to being a seeker, Reid, be a dweller. Your dwelling will save you from the unproductive restlessness that seekers sometimes fall into.

For your search I offer you two seekers who are dear to my heart, Nikos Kazantzakis and Simone Weil. Nikos was a wonderfully passionate Greek who lived as one with wings. He could not slow down. He lived hunting for God. In his autobiography, *Report to Greco*, he is talking with an old monk at the Sinai Monastery. The topic of the conversation is his terrible restlessness. He says to the old monk, "I belong to the heresy called, 'always uneasy.' I have been battling ever since childhood."

The old monk leans forward, "Battling with whom?" he asks. Nikos hesitates and suddenly feels terror rising in his heart. "With whom?" the old monk asks again, "With God?"

"Yes," Nikos answers, "with God. Can this be a disease? Father, how can I be cured?"

"May you never be cured," the old monk answers. "Since you are wrestling with God, alas if you are ever cured of this disease."[11]

For Nikos this struggle was truly a dis-ease. He spent his life always uneasy, yet wrestling with the Divine. He was not cured of this dis-ease until the great healing of death. His life was a passionate struggle to find God.

The other seeker I offer you is Simone Weil. I suppose we could say she was a Jewish Christian, for she was steeped in Christ. I think the reason Simone found more peace than Nikos is that she learned something Nikos never learned. She learned to wait. Her entire life was a waiting for God. She claims that we can do nothing on our own to get to heaven, but if we wait long enough, God will come and lift us up.

I am especially touched as she describes a mystical experience she had while reading George Herbert's poem "Love." She claims that during one of these recitations Christ came down and took possession of her. Yet even after that experience she struggled with her intellect. Writing of this experience she says:

Yet I still half refused, not my love but my intelligence. For it seemed to me certain, and I still think so today, that one can never wrestle enough with God if one does so out of pure regard for the truth. Christ likes us to prefer truth to him because, before being Christ, he is truth. If one turns aside from him to go toward the truth, one will not go far before falling into his arms.[12]

I give you Nikos and Simone because I think the four of us have a common problem: the need for certitude. Our intellects, dear as they are, can at times be blocks to spiritual growth. Jesus said that it was hard for a rich person to get to heaven. Well, I say that it is hard for an intellectual to fall into the arms of God. But it can happen, as Simone has shown us.

I recall when I was in Jersey you asked me how I could be such a free thinker and still be a Roman Catholic. I pondered, with some amusement, over your question. No matter what church I belong to, there are two things I must hang on to for dear life. One is my head. The other, my heart. Thinking and loving integrate well.

If we claim to be a pilgrim church, we have to be in process. I look at the Roman Catholic church as one in process. I realize the hierarchy in our church don't always seem to be in process. Sometimes they seem to be standing still. But the church is so much larger than the hierarchy. Painful as it is to belong to such a male-dominated church, I find these times exciting. People in the church are discovering they don't need a license to think. Perhaps that is what makes Rome so nervous.

I do not mean to sound flippant about this. For me, the Catholic church is home. This is the place where I have found the most truth. I need the rich traditions of my church. I need her saints and prophets. I need her sacred rites and rich liturgy. I need the rich tradition of meditation and contemplation that I find here. I need the mystical spirituality of this church. I need the Christ I meet in her sacraments. I need her authority that comes from Christ. I love my church very much. That does not mean that all is well, anymore than all is well in our individual families. We are in process, and we are a church of sinners. One of my great concerns about the Catholic church is that until women are given full inclusion in ministry, we will have a terribly incomplete church. Discrimination against women may be more subtle in other churches, but it's there too.

I believe that I have as much a responsibility to challenge the hierarchy of my church as they have to challenge me. It's one boat and Christ is rowing. If I didn't believe that I'd have gotten out a long time ago.

You may find it interesting that Simone Weil came close to crossing the threshold of the Catholic church. Two little words kept her joined instead to "the paste of common humanity." Those words were: *Anathema sit.* She could not imagine a mere mortal saying to anyone: *Anathema sit.* I am with her all the way. I do not believe in excommunication. The only way it would be possible to excommunicate someone would be to prevent them from loving.

I do not mean to sound trite or casual about any of this. Belief is sacred and precious, and there is not enough of it around today. I believe Simone is right. If we search for the truth, along with waiting for God, we are going to fall into the arms of the living God. Don't forget the waiting. And speaking of waiting for God, I must share one last quote from Nikos. This is taken from his reflections on his childhood. It was before he lost his ability to wait.

I remember frequently sitting on the doorstep of our home when the sun was blazing, the air on fire, grapes being trodden in a large house in the neighborhood, the world fragrant with must. Shutting my eyes contentedly, I used to hold out my palms and wait. God always came— as long as I remained a child, He never deceived me—He always came, a child just like myself, and deposited his toys in my hands: sun, moon, wind. "They're gifts," He said, "they're gifts. Play with them. I have lots more." I would open my eyes. God would vanish, but His toys would remain in my hands.[13]

Do you suppose that most of what we need to know to get to heaven we learned as children? Let's keep seeking. Let's keep dwelling. And let's keep waiting for God.

A dweller and a seeker,
Macrina, your sister

I seem to be coming to a point in my life where I see that what the Spirit is demanding of me is only that I be truly present to others.
(Henry)

Henry,

I sat with your words for a long time yesterday. It was a way of being present to myself. I wonder why it is so hard for most of us to be present with the kind of presence that is healing. It does seem to be our vocation as Christians. In my own life I can honestly say that the moments I experience the greatest peace are those moments when I am able to be present with quality. When we bring our whole self to something or someone, we are bringing more than ourself. We are bringing Jesus. We've been told we are temples of the Holy Spirit. I wonder how many of us really believe that in our hearts. It ought to be a truth we wear in our hearts, not just on our lips.

Speaking of the Spirit, I forgot to thank you for lunch last week. It was an uncomfortable and enjoyable lunch. Your words are still heavy in my heart. So you think I need to be more open to and aware of the presence of the Spirit in my life? What can I say? Your words spent a painful afternoon with me. At first I felt angry and hurt.

But when I got home, I really prayed about what you said and a deep peace came to me. I decided I was pretty lucky to have a friend who loved me enough to take the risk of calling me to a deeper spiritual life. Friends who do that for me are quite rare. I know you say this to me because you see how God is using me in the lives of others and you want me to be emptier and more aware that it is God's work being done. You know me pretty well. I do put up a lot of blocks. As I pray today, I am so aware that there is a part of me that needs to be healed of my fear of really turning my life over to God in complete trust and letting Jesus be my life. It is control I don't like to let go of.

You know how I long to be a good monk and to live counterculturally, but everywhere I compromise. I still depend far too much on human beings. It seems so difficult to put my trust entirely in God. I am comforted by the fact that Thomas Merton struggled with the same thing. His words in *The Sign of Jonas* could be my very own. He says, "Lord, I have not lived like a monk, like a contemplative. The first essential is missing. I only say I trust you. My actions prove that the one I trust is myself— and that I am still afraid of you."[14] I identify so much with Thomas Merton. He too was a restless soul. He longed for his hermitage, but he didn't really find peace there. If peace isn't in our hearts, we won't find it in our hermitages. How I long to be at home in the hermitage of my heart! I have dreams even in these days when asceticism isn't a popular word, of finding the strength for long night vigils and discovering my knees again.

I feel vulnerable today. My desire to center has not driven away my restless spirit. Yet all this is a part of life, and I know I must bear both the burden and the grace of my personality. I am such an airhead at times and though it often gives me grief, at other times I think it quite becomes me.

Concerning the loneliness we spoke of, mine is vast. It is a kind of infinite sadness that no human being can ever fill. It is everyone's sadness though not everyone gives it a name. Although we can never be fully cured of this infinite sadness until we are totally united with God, the healing presence that you spoke of in your letter does give comfort along the way.

Macrina

I hope you do not lose the fruits of your desert experience. It would be a shame to let the world creep in and smother what you

have worked so hard to achieve. Remember that the author of *The Cloud* keeps referring to contemplation as one's "work." I'm finally recognizing what that means. Prayer requires dedication. Nothing of value comes easy. I believe we must all work hard to keep things in perspective. At times I think I, too, need a desert experience. But how to fit it into an active life! Is it possible to have a contemplative experience while constantly engaged in the fight? How can one incorporate one's secular work with the work of prayer?

(Richard)

Dear Richard,

Your letter was welcomed by the questions in my own heart. If there is no possibility for a deep prayer life for active people, what hope is there for any of us? Those of us who have gone away to desert places or joined monastic communities to seek God often wake up and discover that we, too, are in the fast lane. It is a sad awakening and a sin I'd rather not confess, but it is true, and so your remarks about not letting the world creep in and smother the fruits of my desert experience are well taken. The most important fruit of my desert experience has been my willingness to take the time to dwell with Christ, in God. The author of *The Cloud* is right. It is a "work." It is also a treasure that I don't want to lose no matter what lane I'm in.

Yes, I think it's possible to have a contemplative experience while engaged in the fight. Perhaps that is part of the wisdom that you, as a university professor, must pass on to others. We will shrivel on the vine unless we learn to dwell. I never cease to be amazed at how comfortable people seem to be with trivia. And yet, my next thought is that their seeming comfort is only a mask. At their inner core I believe most people are crying to connect with God. We will never understand their cries unless we've paid attention to our own cry.

We who have gotten into the fast lane must search for a soul friend. I hesitate using the term *spiritual director* lest we make the mistake of looking for an expert. The desert fathers and mothers were not trained spiritual directors. They were not experts in our terminology, but they were hungry for the Word of

Life and so they sat at the feet and dwelt in the heart of the only expert available, the God of heaven and earth, the Christ who took on our flesh and the Counsellor who was sent to befriend us and teach us.

We must allow ourselves to be taught by God, and we must share with another person our ache for God. We educated people are so afraid to reveal our great emptiness, aren't we? Richard, do you have a soul friend with whom you can comfortably share your spiritual journey? I think this is essential. Search for one.

I must share with you a story about a particularly barren time in my life when I used a tree for a spiritual director. I learned so much that year because I listened in silence. A great famine had swept across my soul and I despaired of finding anyone to walk with me on my spiritual journey. One morning while standing at my east window I noticed two of my friends transplanting a little sycamore tree. Suddenly, I could swear my angel whispered to me, "Let that little sycamore be your soul-friend this year." And I did! I chose a certain time each month to spend time with it. I was far more faithful than I had ever been with other spiritual directors, and it was faithful to me. I developed a great affection for that little tree and watered it through one hot summer. That act of kindness improved our relationship immensely. There were many things I learned from that little sycamore. Time will allow me to share only a few.

Because it was small I couldn't lean on it but could only sit beside it. That taught me a lot about what the role of spiritual guide should be.

Even though it was small, it had the ability to give me a certain amount of shade. You don't have to have a lot of leaves to give shade.

Because it was silent I listened deeply. You don't need a lot of words to connect with God.

When it got thirsty I watered it. The miracle of water is a little like the miracle of God's life. That little sycamore taught me a lot about foot washing. Watering it was a great joy. A soul-friend relationship never works only one way. There is a mutual giving and receiving.

I learned from my tree that being transplanted is possible. I can always put down roots again, connect with the Great Root, and grow on.

What saved me most that year was just my faithfulness in silently being there with my sycamore tree. I couldn't "go out on a limb," like Zacchaeus, to see Jesus because its branches were too small to hold me. Yet its silent presence and faithful shade gave me many glimpses of Jesus.

There were evenings, too, when I stood in need of special protection. I would look out my window at that little sycamore in the moonlight, and I am next to sure its branches were full of angels. Heaven is like that. There will always be someone heaven-sent to "go out on the limb" for me until I am able to make that journey myself. Gazing at that tree full of angels, I began to realize that it wasn't because the tree was too little that I couldn't go out on its limbs. It was because I am too heavy. Now I understand the meaning of the sign in my friend's kitchen that says, "Angels fly because they take themselves lightly." Perhaps leaves fly for the same reason. How hard it is to let go!

I wouldn't recommend using a tree for a spiritual guide all the days of one's life, but that sycamore got me through a long stretch of barrenness. It was only a little tree, and I didn't know it was holy until I spent time with it. Truly, holiness comes wrapped in the ordinary.

Keep searching,
Macrina, your sister

9. Feasting at the Table of Daily Life

There is a table to which we are invited each day. It offers us trees and stones, sunshine and stars, eagles and angels, roots and water, joy and sorrow, earth and fire, flesh and blood, storms and memories, words and silence, spiders and webs, night and day, death and life, crusts, crumbs, and loaves. It is the table that Love prepares for us each moment. It is the table of daily life. Freely we are invited to come and eat.

We do not have to be worthy to be present at this table. We only have to be willing to taste life and let God serve us. To image Love's daily invitation I can think of no better words than George Herbert's poem:

> Love bade me welcome: yet my soul drew back,
>   Guiltie of dust and sinne.
> But quick-ey'd Love, observing me grow slack
>   From my first entrance in,
> Drew nearer to me, sweetly questioning,
>   If I lack'd any thing.
>
> A guest, I answer'd worthy to be here:
>   Love said, You shall be he.
> I the unkinde, ungratefull? Ah my deare,
>   I cannot look on thee.
> Love took my hand, and smiling did reply,
>   Who made the eyes but I?
>
> Truth Lord, but I have marr'd them: let my shame
>   Go where it doth deserve.
> And know you not, sayes Love, who bore the blame?
>   My deare, then I will serve.

You must sit down, sayes Love, and taste my meat:
So I did sit and eat.[1]

Unfortunately, most of us turn away from this table not because we sense our unworthiness, but rather because we are so busy we're oblivious to the invitation. In order for an intimate dialogue such as described in George Herbert's poem to take place, we have to be at least present enough to recognize Love's invitation. I remember a day when this poem became a prayer in me. I was sitting in the Greek Theater at the University of Arkansas. It was very early in the morning just between night and day, and except for God, I was alone. It was an intense and intimate moment to be in such a big place all alone. My heart remembered the words of this poem and suddenly, all unexpected, they were on my lips. I looked at the empty stage and saw Love standing there inviting me. A divine energy quietly invaded me, filled me, surrounded me. This tenderness of God took me by the hand and led me to the table of daily life. I was aware of my unworthiness but this seemed not a problem for God. God asked me only one question in the morning's stillness: "Will you let Love serve you; will you sit and eat?" It was a sacred moment. I sat quietly and let the morning fill me. I prayed the morning. Silently I ate up the dawn. I was feasting at the table of daily life.

Life is enriched by moments such as these. Our experiences feed us all we need to be holy, yet it is only in reflecting on these experiences that they can be changed into prayer.

In this chapter I share with you experiences that have fed me at the table of daily life. Journaling with these experiences has turned them into prayer. It was not a prayer that I was searching for, but rather a prayer that was searching for me. The prayer found me when I accepted Love's invitation to come to the table of life.

A wonderful gift that human beings possess is the ability to feast even on memories from the past. Precious moments from our past that were not understood or cherished at the time can be gathered up, like crumbs, for nourishment in our later years. Thus, lost moments are found again. They are full of grace and can heal us even now. They can be harvested and carried home into our barns.

Everyone receives this invitation to the table of life. It is new every morning. Not everyone welcomes this invitation. We live under the illusion that we are too busy to taste life's moments fully. We allow the noise around us and within us to deafen us to the sounds of life. We are often content to remain shallow. We fail to plumb the depths of all we can be. Busyness, noise, and shallow living are three great enemies of the spiritual life. Flannery O'Connor suggests that human nature is so faulty it can resist any amount of grace, and most of the time it does. To that truth I will add yet another truth giving birth to a paradox. Human nature is so noble that it has the potential to become divine, and sometimes it does.

Each morning as you stand face to face with the grace of the new day, I invite you to proclaim this truth: "I am not too busy to taste the fullness of life today." The choice is yours. The feast is, too!

And now I welcome you to sit with me at the table of life, feasting on the meals that feed me each day. Watch with me as my experiences turn into prayer. Pray with me as I journal with life.

The harvest of healing-rocks and spiderwebs: feasting with childhood memories.

The child within is blessing me today. I see her in the distant fields coming from the wooded thicket, walking slowly toward me. She is myself, the little girl I used to be. She still lives within me. I understand her better now. She was so much wiser than I ever gave her credit for. She stands before me almost healed. She's been to her healing-rock in the woods. It's a wonderful rock with a tablecloth of green moss. And there she sits listening to the running water when her soul needs to have sadness washed away. The sadness doesn't always need to go away. Sometimes it just needs to be understood. Most of the time she goes to her rock to understand.

I think everyone has a place for healing, though they do not always give it a name. As a child I didn't know that rock was my healing-rock. It is only now as I pray with these memories that I realize what was happening at that rock. The rock was the place I went when I was afraid or confused. It was a place of healing for me. It did more to soothe my soul than any confessional.

I remember spending an afternoon at my healing-rock when I discovered the secret of Santa Claus. It was a sad afternoon not because the lie about Santa Claus had been revealed, but because my mind kept drifting back to a question I had once asked my mother. I asked her if there was one Santa Claus for the rich and another for the poor. Although she assured me there was only one, I told her there must be two because the rich kids always got more than the poor. She said that Santa Claus comes to you just the way you are. In my adult life I see the beauty of her answer, but my child's heart was crushed that afternoon in memory of the pain my question must have caused her.

Grown-ups are such funny people, I thought. Why didn't they tell me it was just pretend? All that pain could have been avoided if adults were more comfortable with healthy forms of fantasy. The lies would not have had to be told.

Many an afternoon was spent on my healing-rock meditating on spiders and their daily art exhibit. The spider was one of my favorite childhood images of God. I recall once after a long, boring church service, I told my mother that God was a little like a spider. She thought I was being silly. She didn't ask me to explain my wisdom. On my healing-rock that day I felt liberated from all accusations of silliness as I became aware that my mother just didn't understand what I meant. Being only a child, I didn't have words to explain.

I had acquired a reverential awe for the spider spinning her web. I was certain that my mother had learned how to crochet doilies from watching the spider. She had been to spider school. The web was such a beautiful work of art and if someone came along and destroyed it, with what infinite patience the spider would build it back. How like God! Then one day I heard the passage from John's Gospel being read, "In my father's house there are many mansions . . . and I am going to prepare a place for you." I thought, ". . . many mansions!" Ah, God is just like the spider, weaving many little rooms for us.

With all this pondering over spiders I developed a fondness for webs and could not bear to walk through even a single web thread spun across a walkway. To this day you may, on some morning, see me bend low as I walk the hill to Morning Praise. I go under webs instead of through them. I am not ashamed of this bit of sentimentality left over from childhood. I have bowed low for lesser beauties. If it takes a spider to teach me to bow, that's fine. At least I am learning.

My childhood meditations held more truth than I could grasp at the time. I am grasping it now. I believe there is a Great Weaver in the heavens, and she is slowly spinning a web that will make heaven and earth one. Let's not break the sacred web.

The harvest of blessings: feasting with what's left behind and what goes ahead of you.

To bless a person, place, or thing means to leave a little bit of yourself with them. To bless is to leave some of your energy, your power, your goodness and mercy behind you, or to send it on ahead.

I have been blessed so often in my lifetime. Now it is time for me to let my own goodness and kindness pursue others.

I love the memory of the woman with the flow of blood creeping up behind Jesus and touching the hem of his garment. The story goes that Jesus knew she had touched him because power went out of him. He had blessed her, and he felt his blessing going forth. I would like to take the story a bit further and suggest that when the woman touched him he also felt energy coming in. He felt her blessing. Can you imagine what it felt like after a hard week of ministry to find at least one person of faith, to find someone so believing that she was willing to touch just his garment's hem?

I am certain that Jesus felt blessed. He was blessed by a woman whom society had cast out. Oh, the beauty of that moment! She blessed Jesus with her faith. He blessed her with healing. She blessed him with her touch. He blessed her with acceptance. It was a marvelous exchange! Blessing for blessing! Goodness and kindness were pursuing both Jesus and the woman. What a moment of blessing! The woman left a part of herself with Jesus. And Jesus left a part of himself with her.

I want to learn how to bless like that. I want to leave a bit of myself, for the glory of God, wherever I go. This morning as I walked along the beach at Malibu I looked at all the footprints in the sand. I prayed for the owners of those footprints. They were blessings in the sand. "God," I prayed, "do you know whose footprints these are? Would you fill these persons' lives with meaning? Please teach them to choose the things in life that really matter." I touched the footprints tenderly as I spoke to God. A line from a poem by Coleridge that I once scribbled in my journal came to mind: "A stream of love burst from my heart, and I blessed them unaware."

I know the tide will come and wash these prints into the sea. But this time it will be different. This time it will be prayers and blessings going out to sea, and all because I took the time to be present to those footprints. I left a part of myself with those prints, and the owners of the footprints, all unknowing, left a bit of presence with me. And God looked with love on the owners of those footprints as they faded into the sea.

The harvest of love: feasting with the call to love.

What does it mean to love? How do we spread this table in our hearts? If *love* suffers from overuse as a word, it suffers from underuse as a virtue. I would so like for my love to bear at least some faint resemblance to the love of Jesus. In my meditations this morning my thoughts return to Sister Maggie, who died last year at the age of eighty-three. On the morning of the day she died she walked into our superior's office and asked an amazing question. "How do you love?" she asked. Sister Louise wasn't prepared for this one. Maggie was the kind of person who often came with a long list of complaints. Perhaps this brand new question came out of an ache she had carried with her all these years. How do you love? What a wonderful question to still be asking when you're eighty-three years old. What a wonderful question to be asking on the day you die.

Sister Louise spoke to Maggie about the love of Jesus, pointing out to her some of the ways Jesus loved. And then Sister Maggie burst forth with a cry of the heart that would probably be our own cry if we were able to check the depths of our hearts. "Oh," she said, "I want to love. I want to love like that." She died that evening.

I have a vision of God hearing her cry and saying, "If she wants to love she's not going to learn it here, so I'll take her to my own heart." Perhaps that isn't the best of publicity for those of us who were her sisters, but I suspect it's the story of our lives.

What do we see when we look into our families, our communities, our hearts? What do we see when we look into the faces of our parents, our sisters and brothers, our friends? Let's not wait until we're eighty-three to ask, "How do you love?" Are we teaching one another what love is? I'm not sure of very much in life. I don't have a lot of ready answers, and I still do much wondering and pondering, but there's one thing of which I am certain. WE OUGHT NOT DIE UNTIL WE LEARN TO LOVE. Life doesn't work without love.

The harvest at the shopping mall: feasting with the shoppers.

My restlessness drove me to the mall today. There I milled around among all the shoppers looking at things I didn't need and wanting to fill up my emptiness by purchasing some useless item. Suddenly something within me brought a poignant awareness of all the people rushing through the mall. It was as though in the midst of this crowded mall something holy was oozing through these scurrying human beings. I felt a sacred urge to kneel down in their midst and bow my head in honor of all the beauty of their lives that goes unseen. I overcame this urge rather quickly lest I be trampled by the scurrying mob or locked up for being mentally unbalanced. We must, after all, follow the normal majority. I did manage to find a bench nearby where I sat down and had "long looks" at the people. The long looks became prayers. I prayed the people as they rushed, casting healing glances in their direction.

O God, I prayed, these are the people made in your image. Do you rush like this, God? Do you hurry through the heavens looking for bargains? O God, be in every heart that hurries. Be in every step that people take. Help them to know what it is they are shopping for. Feed the hungers of their hearts with a food they'll never find in shopping malls. Help them to slow down so they can taste their true hunger.

While still gazing at these hurrying people, I had a strange and lovely dream for them. I dreamed that everyone in the mall suddenly fell to their knees and adored the God in each other. A strange dream, perhaps, but wouldn't it be powerful if it came true? Can you imagine the peace of such a moment? Everyone in the shopping mall, kneeling, gazing at the image of God in one another! Can you hear this moment of quiet? Can you see this moment of holiness? Can you imagine how heaven would feel?

I roused myself from my dream, got up slowly, and walked through the crowds back to the car, back to the solitude of my cell. I had bought nothing. My hands were empty, but my heart was full.

The harvest of fog: feasting on a foggy morning.

This morning my life was folded in prayer. The image that comes to mind in describing my mountain drive in thick fog, is the memory of my mother making meringue for lemon pie. I see her beating the egg whites until suddenly they become a mountain of whiteness. Little mountain peaks completely cover the field of yellow.

The field I started out with this morning was a field of green along with a whole array of other colors. As I climbed the curvy mountainous road, the field of green soon became covered over with a cloud of white mountains. The fog came rolling in and enfolded me. I thought of William Blake's tree full of angels and Mama's meringue. The first symbol seemed protective; the second, nourishing. Since this was a dangerous road, I decided to pray with the protective symbol. I imaged God sending an entire legion of angels to guide me across the mountains. Now and then I would see tips of tree branches piercing the mountain of whiteness. God has sent me not only a tree full of angels, I thought. I have been given hundreds of trees full of angels—a mountain of angels. What a terrible beauty! Terrible because I was not able to see well. A beauty because that is the only suitable word to describe a mountain of angels.

Then suddenly I thought, "I can see! It's just the things far away that I can't see. I see what is nearby." So often in life these things that are close at hand are the very ones I miss. They're the crumbs that cannot nourish me because I'm looking off into the distance. I began to pray the things close at hand: the shield of fog, a tiny patch of road, treasures of nature faintly pushing through the fog, the car, and myself.

It occurred to me, as I prayed with what was visible to my eye in the midst of these mountains enveloped in fog, that not

even fog can hide God's radiant identity. Pieces of a poem by
Edna St. Vincent Millay that I memorized years ago came to
me. I prayed:

> O God . . . no dark disguise
> Can e're hereafter hide from me
> Thy radiant identity!
> Thou canst not move across the grass
> But my quick eyes will see Thee pass,
> Nor speak, however silently,
> But my hushed voice will answer Thee.
> I know the path that tells Thy way
> Through the cool eve of every day;
> God, I can push the grass apart
> And lay my finger on Thy heart![2]

In my foggy morning prayer, I, too, discovered that I could
push the fog apart, reach through the clouds, and touch God's
heart.

The harvest of stormy weather: feasting on a storm.

Today I felt rather empty and unvisited by God. Then about
two o'clock in the afternoon, after I had prayed for the hun-
dredth time, "O when will You come?" God came. God came
in a storm, a wonderful storm that bent everything to the
ground in adoration. The Great Spirit has a way of bending us
when we forget to adore. While the lightning is flashing and
crashing, the trees bending to the ground in adoration, men
and women are at least aware that something majestic and extreme is being celebrated in their midst. With each storm the
peoples of the earth may fall to the ground in adoration, stand
in awe and silence, or fall to their knees in fright. Regardless of
which position we take, at least God has gotten our attention.
The extremely unenlightened do not even notice God's presence
in the storm.

O Great and Unnameable Source of Life, I pray to you: When I forget to adore, please send me a storm. If it takes flashes of light and peals of thunder to get my attention, then send me a storm.

The harvest of suffering: feasting with the daily news.

I clasp the newspaper to my heart like a Bible. I weep over the tragedy of human life. My candle flickers in the darkness of the night. I am trying for an hour of vigil for my dear broken world.

God, my life is here before you like clay, but I don't feel very pliable. I feel angry. This morning with Psalm 102 I prayed, "The children of those who serve you shall dwell secure" (NJB). I smiled a cynical smile. I like to take the Scriptures seriously, but God, we both know this isn't true. In the shadows of this night I try to make some sense of this Psalm message. So many people who serve you do not dwell secure, and neither do their children. I glance again at the paper. I see the poverty, the wars, the enslavements of the human person. I see, in many instances, the injustice people have to suffer simply because they are trying to serve you. I see the immense helplessness that so many people experience in the face of unjust systems. I see people getting rich from other people's miseries. I ache because of all the doors that are closed in people's faces every day. And I say to you, "What's happening to their prayers, God? Are you using their prayers for a carpet in heaven? Well, they aren't in heaven. These people need for you to lean down from heaven. The people who are crying out to you are still in Egypt. It is time to split the sea again. It is time to save."

We are the people who claim to have been made in God's image. I can hardly look at what we've done to that image. I see the misery human beings suffer, and I say in regard to all this: "It is enough! It is enough, God! Where do you hang out when your people are starving?"

In the shadows of this dark night, I seem to see God leaning from heaven again. This time God comes not as a tiny, helpless child but as a sorrowing, desperate parent, and God repeats to the human race my own agonizing cry, "It is enough! How long must I wait for you to put on the mind of Christ? How long must I wait for you to live in my image? What are you doing with the prayers of your brothers and sisters? Are you making them into plush carpets for your own feet to rest on?"

I've never been very good at feasting on the daily newspaper. It turns bitter in my mouth. And yet, this is my world. This face of suffering I must embrace as a part of my responsibility. Part of the feast is becoming aware of the world that is mine. Part of the feast is owning this broken world as my own brokenness. I clasp the newspaper to my heart and ask once again in the stillness of the night, "What are we doing to the image of God in one another?"

The harvest of the Incarnation: feasting on a mystery.

It seems to me that the mystery of the Incarnation ought to be celebrated every day, not just at Christmas. It is that moment when God chose to help us understand that our flesh is holy by taking it on himself. He wrapped himself in our flesh. The Word became flesh!

What a day for earth! The Word of God came bounding into the midst of a desperate land. It stood on the earth yet touched the heavens, and everywhere it fell it filled the earth with the danger and the beauty that comes from being so close to God.

It was the spirit of the living God sent from heaven into the womb of Mary. Out of all that leaping, bounding, and hovering, a child was born, one called Jesus. And God's forceful, leaping spirit stirred within this child just as she had once stirred the waters when the world was yet waking.

Slowly God's holy spirit awakened Jesus to know that he was sent to stand on the earth while touching the heavens, and to teach us to do the same. What a day for earth! The day God leaned from heaven! We call it Incarnation. It is a gentle memory in our hearts. God chose to wear our frail human flesh to help us recognize our splendor. Why else did this Word bound from heaven except to establish a relationship with us?

Climbing down through the stars
to the stars on earth
The divine face meshing with the human
Heaven touching earth
We call it Incarnation!

You came as a star
led by a star
through the stars
to the stars
We never knew we were stars
until you came.

O God, we welcome you
We lovingly share our frail human flesh
and our starry planet with you
We wrap you in our flesh
We embrace you with joy
as you reach out your hands and your heart
to become one of us.

It was Mary who first wrapped you
    in our human flesh
Her womb, the first altar
consecrated from all eternity
to be your first earthly home.

How holy is this earth!
Your glory streamed through our lives
    like stars
the day you leaned from heaven
You came to help us see our glory
Following the star
we lean into your glory
In your light, we see the light

We never knew we were stars
until you came.

In the depths of my heart where God teaches me wisdom,
I'm finally able to own the truth that God leaned down from
heaven to show us how good we are, rather than to tell us how
bad we are. To save sinners, yes, but above all to save us from
the folly of our own self-hate. We have heard far too much
about the bad news of our corruption. The good news is that
our frailty is what God chose to be enthroned in during his
sojourn on earth. It is an incredible compliment to us. God
loved us enough to get inside our skin. God loved us enough
to help us see our dignity and value. We are like stars. Our
light is the reflection of a greater light. We are beautiful to
behold when we let God shine on us, in us, and through us.

The feast of Christmas is the feast of God's leaning down
from heaven to become one of us. It was an awesome moment
in history. It is still awesome to know that we are called to be
divinized. Every Christmas and every day the message comes
home a little stronger. God has pitched a tent in our hearts. We
are dwelling places for the Beloved, the Source of Life. What a
day for earth! The day God leaned from heaven!

The harvest of good-bye: feasting on the last week at a cherished place.

It was a wonderful day filled with tears and peace. It all
began with my morning prayer. I was praying with the first
letter of Peter and was blessed with these words: "Should anyone ask you the reason for this hope of yours, be ever ready to
reply . . ." I stopped reading in order to taste my hope more
deeply. It is true. A pervading hope that I can't always explain
lingers in my soul. And though I am leaving this cherished
place where I have lived for four years, the hope will leave with
me.

It was a stormy morning. I welcomed it joyfully, because in
spite of the hope, I felt a bit stormy inside. It was good of God

to dress up the morning to fit my mood. Everyone who lives here is gone today. It is a wonderful gift to my solitude: an empty house, morning, and me. I sat down and brought some of the people I'll be leaving into my prayer: Marietta and Rueben, Paul and Theresa, Joe and Anne Marie, Tami, Janine, Gary and Greg, William, Julie, Catherine, Xavier, Alice, Joe. They filed through my mind and heart into the heart of God. I blessed them and let them go. I ached at letting them go, yet I did it willingly. I leave places well. I think it has something to do with my pilgrim state and my spirit remembering another land. Still, would it not be a treason if I didn't ache a little as I go? Robert Frost comes to pray with me and I say:

> Ah, when to the heart of man
> Was it ever less than a treason
> To go with the drift of things,
> To yield with a grace to reason,
> And bow and accept the end
> Of a love or a season?[3]

I moved to the window in the den where the mourning dove has her nest. The storm was still raging. Balancing my coffee cup on the window ledge, I meditated on the mourning dove. I looked at her sitting on that nest, faithfully believing in the eggs. She was being tossed to and fro by the wind, her feathers drenched with rain. I felt so unfaithful in contrast to her. Do I believe in my community as much as she believes in those eggs? When the storms blow me around, what do I do? My questions stopped and I decided that I, too, am strangely faithful. I looked at her again and prayed for her. Why not?

This afternoon I started packing. I've been throwing things away with a passion. I wish it were as easy to clean up the inside of my life, to throw away my rebellious spirit, my selfishness, my pride and control, my pettiness. The packing continued. I sat down in the midst of my clutter, had a glass of wine, and thought about the Ascension. The Feast of the Ascension is so present to me this year. Unless I go away, the spirit will not come. I do feel that unless I go from here, the spirit cannot do a new thing in my life. And a new thing is wanting to be done. I hear it asking for birth. Who am I to say no to birth?

I think I've loved it here more than any other place I've ever been, and yet I feel the same about other places. I love them all the best. I love ministry. I love being a facilitator of life.

I am asking you, God, to guard me this week under the shadow of your wings (me and the mourning dove). Keep me from all forms of self-pity. Help me to minister to the end. Keep my hope burning brightly. And should anyone ask me the reason for this hope of mine, I'll be ever ready to explain. It's the life we can't see yet that keeps me and the mourning dove in the nest, hoping. It is in our instincts and spirits that something precious is within our reach. They call us co-creators.

The harvest of darkness: feasting with a dried-up heart.

Today, my God, I am asking you to bring back my heart from wherever it has wandered. My enthusiasm has waned. I feel like a dried-up brook. I reach for the hem of your garment. I can't find it. Yet even in this darkness you have prepared a feast. The feast is one of remembering the days of old when my brook was gushing with life. The feast is a reminder that there will always be a bit of solid ground to stand on or wings to fly with. The feast is a wonderful quote that I found in my mailbox today, exactly the tonic to help me celebrate the darkness. This anonymous quote, found in the home of David Larson, M.D., says:

When we walk to the edge of all the light we have and take that step into the darkness of the unknown, we must believe that one of two things will happen . . . There will be something solid for us to stand on, or we will be taught to fly.

Ah! What a song for my straying heart! Yes, the beautiful thing about this darkness is that it has not prevented me from coming to the table of daily life with wide-open eyes. If it is darkness I must eat, I will eat it with reverence. For I know that in the middle of this darkness I will be given solid ground or wings.

Yet as I pray to you these days, I miss my heart. Do you know where it is? Have you seen it, my God? My poet's heart has dried up. It is gone. There is nothing left. That part of me that could see in the dark is gone. That part of me that could still feel when all the world had turned to ashes is gone.

So what is left on this barren spring day? What is left of the poet's heart? A tiny ray of hope that comes from remembering! That's all that's left, but it's enough to begin the feast.

I remember the days when I held the hands of those who were stumbling, always able to show them another path or point out another star. I remember being able to pick up another's heart and hold it during the dry seasons. But today I can't find enough of my own heart to pick up the heart of another. The poet in me has gone to some sad brook where the waters are dried up. The only ray of hope left is that the brook still remembers that the waters have been there. The parched ground remembers as it looks to the heavens. It is waiting as all lovers must wait. The parched ground is my heart and it, too, remembers that the waters have been there. Never say that all is lost. It is remembering that blesses and saves us. My poet's heart may be gone today, but I have enough vision left. I have enough memory left to feast for a long, long time. And if things get really bad on this once-solid ground, I think I could learn to fly.

The harvest of seeking: feasting with the search.

I am seeking you, God. The great hunt is on, and though I tremble at the thought of seeing you face to face, I search anew each day with a passion that will not wear out. I breathe in. I breathe out. Do I breathe you in and out? I wonder quietly. Then I wonder if you are in my wondering. I begin to roam through the cave of my heart searching desperately. I feel warm and know that I'm getting close to you. I peer within, longingly. Then I fear that you are in my peering. I get nervous, realizing that you are terribly near. You are moving in on me. You are seeking me as much as I am seeking you. It frightens me not to be in control. I change my mind about the seeking. I close my eyes and wait. Do you wait with me in my waiting? When I open my eyes you are gone. O elusive God! Why have you gone away? Is it because I want to be in control of this search?

I do not understand this fruitless search. I feel like a bloodhound on your trail. The scent of you is so near. But when I get you treed, there are no hunters around to help me. I cannot reach you alone. I cannot shoot you from the skies. You refuse to come down. Then just when I think I've found you, you become a nomad again. You are so like your friend Abraham, always on the move, a nomadic, wandering God. You are an ever-moving, always-hiding God.

Or is it otherwise? Am I the one who is moving? Are you the hunter who remains quiet, waiting for the beloved to surrender? O God, throw me a crumb of quiet to soothe my restless, wandering heart. I am tired of seeking you. I know that I'll find you on the day I allow myself to be found by you. But I am not that tame yet. Please, God, respect my wildness. I am wild, so wild! Beautifully wild! Oh, do not tame this wandering child. But throw me a crumb of quiet, for I am about to lose myself to you and I am scared. It's exactly what you want, I know. But please, God, not yet. I am untamed, and I am seeking, seeking, seeking . . .

The harvest of beauty: feasting with the trees.

A community of empty trees sways outside my window, dancing in the early morning light. Revering them with awe during my morning coffee, I ponder.

How many rays of sunlight have slipped through your wooden fingers, delighting me with golden streams of warmth and awakening me to the new day? How many parties have you hosted for the squirrels, watching their restless little bodies leaping through your limbs—catching them, holding them, and being their support? How often have you welcomed home the birds nesting in your branches, lending them your slender arms, listening to their songs, singing with them as you swayed?

Your green leaves have long ago waved a fond good-bye, returning to the earth to nourish you still more. Yet even in your barrenness, how beautiful you stand! You've held your share of beauty every season, and now with winter's icy breath almost upon you, you seem content. Content as when you wore your coat of green! Content as when you wore your bright and fiery robes! You stand unfretting and untroubled, a community of trees.

In every season you've been here, in every hour, swaying, bowing, bending. You rise up in glory, obeying an inner energy divine. And in this early morning light, I'm in awe. Your presence to me is a mystery deep, telling me stories I've never heard before. I lean forward to catch your rays again. Such golden designs you send into this room.

A community of trees! A contemplative community, making holy space and time. I want to be, like you, a welcome home for every guest. I yearn, like you, to embrace all the colors of my life. I yearn to be the great adorer that you are. To bend and bow and sway! To stand in beauty through all the seasons of my heart!

The harvest of shared bread: feasting at the dinner table.

I am praying about the responsibility I have to those with whom I share bread. Perhaps there's a bit of Judas in us all. I suspect this may be the reason we so seldom reflect on whether we have betrayed the people with whom we sit at table. Do we feel any responsibility to the ones with whom we share bread?

The Hebrew people took quite seriously the event of eating together. They did not lightly break bread with one another.

Would that we could be a bit more careful about eating together, remembering that when we eat together we proclaim that we are friends and can no longer betray one another!

Would that we could put away some of our instant foods and quick methods and spend more time preparing the food, smelling it, and waiting for it! Above all, let us not make a mockery out of the sacredness of the table by eating in front of the television, for like a thief it steals away all hope of quality communion at mealtime.

I believe we are given to one another to help take care of each other, and the table is a wonderful place to begin. It is a place to be nurtured, not only by the food we eat, but through the love and conversation we share with one another, and the stories we tell.

O God, help us not to betray those we sit at table with, whether it be the meal table, the altar, or the table of daily life. Help us to consecrate ourselves as bread for the world as we share this sacred time with one another.

THE HARVEST OF GOD: FEASTING ON YOUR THEOPHANIES

It was only a small wind
    rather gentle, like a breeze.
It blew a strand of hair across my forehead
    and I knew that it was God.

I was awakened by a tiny gleam of light
    it slipped through my curtain, onto my face.
It drew me to my feet and on to the window
    Drawing back the curtains
dawn stepped softly into my room.
    I knew that it was God.

In the middle of my loneliness
    the phone rang.
A voice I knew so well, said
    "Hello, I love you."

Love stirred in my soul
  I knew that it was God.

Rain fell gently on the thirsty ground.
  Slowly, carefully, steadily it came
to an earth parched with waiting.
  Through those holy raindrops
I walked, unafraid - without an umbrella.
  I knew that it was God.

It was only a little bitterness I thought
  but it wouldn't leave my heart.
It hung around my soul for ages
  until a storm came, violent and terrifying.
It shook me to the depths of my being
  and blew all the bitterness away.
I knew that it was God.

It was only a Silver Maple
  but in the morning's sunlight
It was filled with heaven.
  I stood in a trance
as one touched by angel wings.
  I knew that it was God.

O God, I cried,
  Endearing One, I love you!
You cannot hide from me.
  Between the cracks of daily life
I find you waiting
  to be adored.
You slip into my life
  like night and day
  like stars and sunshine.
I know that you are God.

NOTES

Chapter 2: Frail and Glorious

1. Dietrich Bonhoeffer, *The Cost of Discipleship* (New York: Macmillan, 1963), 45, 46.
2. Graham Greene, *The Power and the Glory* (New York: Viking Press, 1948), 283, 284.
3. Raoul Plus, S.J., *Dust Remember Thou Art Splendor* (New York: Frederick Pustet, 1941), 15.
4. Thomas Merton, "The Victory," *Collected Poems* (New York: New Directions, 1946), 115.

Chapter 4: The Prayer of a Woman Who Understood Crumbs

1. The story of the Canaanite woman, Matt. 15:21–28, Mark 7:24-30 is taken from the Revised Standard Version of the Bible, Catholic edition (Toronto: Thomas Nelson & Sons, 1966).

Chapter 5: Into the Eye of God

1. Guigo II, *The Ladder of Monks* (Garden City, NY: Doubleday Image Books, 1978), 81, 82.
2. Dom Marmion, *Union with God*, trans. Mother Mary St. Thomas (St. Louis: B. Herder, 1949), 184.

Chapter 6: A Handful of Flour, a Little Oil

1. Anthony de Mello, *The Song of the Bird*, (Anand, India: Gujarat Sahitya Prakash, 1982) 14.

Chapter 7: A Tree Full of Angels

1. Thornton Wilder, *Our Town* (1938, 1957; reprint, New York: Harper & Row, 1968), 99, 100.
2. William Blake, "The Tyger," *The Poetry and Prose of William Blake*, ed. David V. Erdman (Garden City, NY: Doubleday, 1970), 24.
3. Blake, "Auguries of Innocence," op. cit., 481.
4. Leon Bloy, *The Woman Who Was Poor*, trans. J. J. Collins (London: Sheed & Ward, 1947), 355.
5. Johannes Metz, *Poverty of Spirit*, trans. John Drury (New York: Paulist, 1968), 3.
6. *The Cloud of Unknowing*, newly edited, introduction by William Johnston (Garden City, NY: Doubleday Image Books, 1973), 146.

7. Angelus Silesius (Johannes Scheffler), *The Cherubinic Wanderer*, trans. Maria Shrady (New York: Paulist, 1986), 77.
8. C. S. Lewis, *Mere Christianity*, (New York: Macmillan, 1960), 120.
9. Etty Hillesum, *An Interrupted Life* (New York: Pocket Books, 1985), 195.
10. Ibid., 238.
11. Marilyn Schwab, *A Gift Freely Given* (Mt. Angel, Or: Benedictine Sisters, 1986), 39.
12. Thomas Merton, *The Sign of Jonas* (Garden City, NY: Doubleday Image Books, 1956), 243.
13. Thomas Merton, *New Seeds of Contemplation* (New York: New Directions, 1972), 53.
14. Nikos Kazantzakis, *Report to Greco* (New York: Simon & Schuster, 1965), 293
15. Emily Dickinson, *Selected Poems of Emily Dickinson* (New York: The Modern Library, 1924), 170.
16. Rabindranath Tagore, *Gitanjali* (New York: Macmillan, 1978), 35.
17. The *Philokalia*, vol. 1, trans. G. E. H. Palmer, Philip Sherrard, and Kallistos Ware (London: Faber & Faber, 1979), 254.
18. Julian of Norwich, *Enfolded in Love* (New York: Seabury Press, 1981), 19.
19. John of the Cross, *The Collected Works of John of the Cross*, trans. Kieran Kavanaugh, O.C.D., and Otilio Rodriguez, O.C.D. (Washington, DC: Institute of Carmelite Studies, 1973), 71.
20. Opal Whiteley, *The Story of Opal: The Journal of an Understanding Heart* (Boston: Atlantic Monthly Press, 1920), 62, 63.
21. G. K. Chesterton, *St. Thomas Aquinas* (Garden City, NY: Doubleday Image Books, 1956), 23.

Chapter 8: Finding God in the Mailbox

1. St. Basil, *St. Basil: The Letters*, vol. 1 (New York: G.P. Putnam's Sons, 1926), Letter 12, 105.
2. John Chapman, *John Chapman: Spiritual Letters* (London: Sheed & Ward, 1976), Letter 42, 117.
3. Marmion, *Union with God*, 190.
4. Hillesum, *Interrupted Life*, 263, 264.
5. David Steindl-Rast, *A Listening Heart: The Art of Contemplative Living* (New York: Crossroad, 1983), 30.
6. Lynn Andrews, *Medicine Woman* (New York: Harper & Row, 1983), 128.
7. Whiteley, *Story of Opal*, 166.
8. *Philokalia*, 159, 160.
9. Whiteley, *Story of Opal*, 121.
10. *Peace Pilgrim*, Compiled by the Friends of Peace Pilgrim (Sante Fe: Ocean Tree, 1982), 52.
11. Kazantzakis, *Report to Greco*, 296.
12. Simone Weil, *Waiting for God* (New York: Harper & Row, 1973), 69.
13. Kazantzakis, *Report to Greco*, 44.
14. Merton, *Sign of Jonas*, 82.

Chapter 9: Feasting at the Table of Daily Life

1. George Herbert, "Love (III)," *The Works of George Herbert*, ed. F. E. Hutchinson (Oxford: Clarendon, 1941), 188, 189.
2. Edna St. Vincent Millay, "Renascence," *Collected Poems* (New York: Harper & Row, 1912, 1940, 1956), 12, 13.
3. Robert Frost, "Reluctance," *Collected Poems of Robert Frost* (New York: Holt & Company, 1930), 43.